ANTI-
JAPAN

ANTI-JAPAN

The Politics of Sentiment in Postcolonial East Asia

LEO T. S. CHING

Duke University Press   Durham and London   2019

Library of Congress Cataloging-in-Publication Data
Names: Ching, Leo T. S., [date] author.
Title: Anti-Japan : the politics of sentiment
in postcolonial East Asia / Leo Ching.
Description: Durham : Duke University Press, 2019. |
Includes bibliographical references and index.
Identifiers: LCCN 2018044268 (print)
LCCN 2018059395 (ebook)
ISBN 9781478003359 (ebook)
ISBN 9781478001881 (hardcover : alk. paper)
ISBN 9781478002895 (pbk. : alk. paper)
Subjects: LCSH: East Asia—Relations—Japan. |
Japan—Relations—East Asia. | East Asia—
Relations—United States. | United States—Relations—
East Asia. | Japan—Foreign public opinion, East Asian.
| United States—Foreign public opinion, East Asian. |
World War, 1939–1945—Influence. | Nationalism—
Japan—History. | Imperialism—History—20th century.
Classification: LCC DS518.45 (ebook) |
LCC DS518.45 .C46 2019 (print) | DDC 303.48/25052—dc23
LC record available at https://lccn.loc.gov/2018044268

Cover art: Anti-Japanese protesters at the Bell Tower
Hotel, Xi'an, China. September 15, 2012. Courtesy of
BBBar / Alamy.

Publication of this open monograph
was the result of Duke University's
participation in TOME (Toward
an Open Monograph Ecosystem),
a collaboration of the Association
of American Universities, the
Association of University Presses,
and the Association of Research
Libraries. TOME aims to expand the
reach of long-form humanities and
social science scholarship including
digital scholarship. Additionally, the
program looks to ensure the sustain-
ability of university press monograph
publishing by supporting the highest
quality scholarship and promoting a
new ecology of scholarly publishing
in which authors' institutions bear
the publication costs. Funding from
Duke University Libraries made it
possible to open this publication to
the world.

For Thanh

CONTENTS

In August 2017, four Chinese men dressed in Second World War Japanese military uniforms posed at the Continental Bank Warehouse in Shanghai where Chinese troops fought the Japanese imperial army in 1937. In February 2018, two different men, also in Japanese military garb, struck various poses in front of a memorial site on Zijin Mountain in Nanjing where Chinese civilians were murdered by the Japanese army, also in 1937. The images went viral and predictably garnered strong and mostly negative reactions from netizens and unleashed a flood of criticisms against these youths in both mainstream and new media. The situation has escalated to the extent that China's top legislative body, citing the Zijin case as an example, is proposing a "heroes and martyrs protection law" to punish people who "glorify wars or acts of invasion." Even the Chinese foreign minister, Wang Yi, joined the fray by calling them "scums among the Chinese people" (Huang 2018). What upsets the netizens and politicians alike, I surmise, is not only that these men dressed up as Japanese soldiers but also that they deliberately posed in front of memorial sites of Japanese aggression and Chinese resistance that formed the foundation of postwar anti-Japanism.

The uproar caused by these incidents also inspired a new neologism in cyberspace: *jing-ri* (精日), literally, "spiritually Japanese," an abbreviation of *jing-shen-ribenren*, or Chinese people who identify themselves spiritually with the Japanese. The premise is that these misguided youths' minds have been contaminated by Japan and, more importantly, they lacked proper understanding of Sino-Japanese history. The term is widely debated on Chinese websites, especially in relation to another term, *ri-za* (日杂), or "Japanized mongrel." To many, the two phrases represent different degrees of affinity with Japan: the latter is a more radical or extreme form of the former. What is striking but unsurprising in the media coverage and online discussions of these incidents is the resort to normative nationalist discourse of collective shaming and the blame of historical amnesia. Two decades of state-led patriotic education and countless anti-Japanese TV dramas certainly couldn't have anticipated the emergence of these *jing-ri* or *ri-za* elements in Chinese society!

The emergence of these acts and their accompanying neologisms, this book will argue, represent a shift of geopolitics whereby modern/colonial Japanese hegemony is giving way to the rise of China. This transimperial moment also signals the complete incorporation of China into global capitalism and the growing influence of Japanese popular culture despite official censorship and bans. The shift of global hegemony is always uneven, contradictory, and, at times, violent. While China has overtaken Japan as the world's second largest economy, its cultural influence, especially in the realm of popular culture, lags far behind Cool Japan and the Korean Wave. It is noteworthy that some of the *jing-ri* offenders first tried out their Japanese uniforms in an animation convention where cosplaying well-known anime characters is a major part of fandom all over the world today. We should also attend to the prevalent new mediascape that continues to blur the line between virtuality and reality and the desire to seek attention and confirmation via multiple social media platforms. In a WeChat post attributed to one of the alleged cosplayers in front of the Warehouse in Shanghai, he describes in detail their successful "mission" and the "thrill" of photographing in the location at night before the watchful eyes of bystanders (Cao 2018).

The emergence of the *jing-ri* discourse certainly complicates the dominant anti-Japanism in Chinese society today. When I taught a session about popular culture in East Asia at Duke Kunshan University in spring 2017, I was surprised by the Chinese students' familiarity and fluency with Japanese (and Korean) popular culture. They not only find ways to hop over the great firewall of China, but they also find much of Japanese popular culture translated and mediated through Taiwan and Hong Kong. Many of them are *jing-ri* but not in the spiritual definition of the word, but, as in its other meanings, to be skilled or proficient, in things about Japan. However, when I asked some of these students if there's another anti-Japan protest, what would they do, many of them said they will, without hesitation, march on the streets. These students clearly separate consumption from identity: consuming Japanese commodities and culture does not mean that they are becoming Japanese. The reaction to the Japanese military cosplay and the students' maneuvering between consumption and activism point to both the limits and relevance of nationalism today. Pro- and anti-Japanism need to be apprehended in their complexity, contradictions, and particular historical conjunctures. It is this messiness of the trans-imperial moment that the book is trying to address.

I began tracking anti-Japan demonstrations in the spring of 2005, largely due to personal reasons. I was making preliminary plans to take my then seven-year-old son to visit my father's grave in Dandong, just outside of Shenyang city in northeastern China. It would have been my wife and son's first trip to my father's hometown. I visited there with my mother for the first time in 1988 to bring over his remains after he passed away in Japan. It was a trip of great importance to my mother, who still lives in Japan and has since remarried a Japanese man. It has always bothered her that while she and I had made occasional visits, her grandson has never met his long-distance relatives. Our plan brought her much joy and excitement. The only decision needed to be made was whether we would go through Japan first and travel together or simply meet up with her in China.

Then came the April anti-Japan demonstrations.

As the protests spread across several cities and amassed tens of thousands of people, anxious phone calls from my mother came more frequently. When a good-sized demonstration took place in Shenyang on April 17, 2005, my mother pressed the panic button and announced that the trip was off. She simply did not think it was safe for us to travel to China, despite my assurance that the protests would subside by the time we arrived and the obvious fact that we are not Japanese. She was not convinced. Images of violence and fury transmitted through the television screen were too vivid and immediate for her. My stepfather, a man who has experienced both the impoverishment of war defeat and the abundance of postwar economic growth, was obviously disturbed and perturbed by the demonstrations. He asked me on the phone incredulously: "Why do they still hate us? The war has long been over. Japan is a peace-loving country now. Why are they still so angry?"

The protests had subsided almost completely by the end of April. We, however, decided to postpone our travel until the summer. My stepfather's seemingly genuine and naïve query, however, remained with me: "Why do they hate us?" "Why do they hate us?" has reverberation in the post-9/11 American consciousness. In an interesting way, anti-Japanism and anti-Americanism converge on the question of identity and difference, us and them. For George W. Bush, "they" are simply haters of freedom and democracy; for Koizumi Jun'ichirō, "they" are merely Japan bashers who intend to endanger bilateral relations. For both leaders, "they" become an incommensurable difference that only serves to reconsolidate the self-assured identity of the "us." What is lacking is any attempt at self-reflexivity on how the other is constituted through the actions of the self. Despite the myopia and ignorance of the political leaders, "Why do they hate us?" as an emotive response to anti-Japanism and anti-Americanism can become a crucial point of departure for critical thinking. Once we can shed the self-pity and innocence implied in the question "Why do they hate us?" we can move toward the politics of reconciliation.

It is impossible to acknowledge all the people who have provided opportunities for me to share some of the ideas presented in this book. I am grateful for their advice, criticism, and support. I thank the late Nancy Abelmann, Yan Hairong, Robert Tierney, Masamichi Inoue, Douglas Shoemaker, Shu-mei Shih, Katsu Endo, Cody Poulton, Richard King, the late Arif Dirlik, Kuan-Hsing Chen, Chua Beng Huat, Tomiyama Ichirō, Komagome Takeshi, Itagaki Ryūta, Soyoung Kim, Huang Mei-er, Ping hui Liao, Michael Bourdaghs, Ya-chung Chuang, Mariam B. Lam, Younghan Cho, John Treat, Lila Kurnia, Hyunjung Lee, Michael Berry, Rob Wilson, and many others. I thank both Reynolds Smith for helping me to clarify my thinking and writing and Ken Wissoker for his unwavering support and guidance. And I offer my gratitude to the two anonymous readers for their critical engagement and patience.

Part of chapter 2 was previously published in *Sino-Japanese Transculturation: From the Late Nineteenth Century to the End of the Pacific War*, ed. Richard King, Cody Poulton, and Katsuhiko Endo (Lanham, MD: Lexington Books, 2012); portions of chapter 4 and chapter 6 have appeared in *Cultural Studies* 26, no. 5 (2012) and *boundary 2* 45, no. 3 (2018), respectively.

INTRODUCTION. Anti-Japanism (and Pro-Japanism) in East Asia

An early scene from *Bodyguards of the Last Governor* (1996; dir. Alfred Cheung), a satire on the impending 1997 handover of Hong Kong to mainland China, depicts a night rally against Japan. The outgoing British governor with his family in the motorcade is startled by the noise of a commotion. The camera pans across a crowd of seated protesters listening to a speech by a Hong Kong politician. Waving signs that read "Down with Japanese Militarism!" and "Diaoyu Islands Belong to China!" and repeating the politician's chants of "Boycott Japanese goods!" and "Down with Japanese imperialism!" the crowd is orderly and enthusiastic. Amid the bustle, Lugo, who will become one of the bodyguards for the British-anointed last governor as a parting joke, shouts down the names of popular Japanese celebrities in 1990s Hong Kong, such as Kimura Takuya and Miyazaki Rie, and gives a satisfying grin to his wife sitting next to him. The camera then cuts to the politician who is now offstage. A female aide comes to his side and says that he must be tired and offers him some sushi for sustenance, of which he gladly partakes. The politician gets back on the stage and urges the crowd to toss away any clothing that is made in Japan. As others hurl away their socks, shoes, and so forth, Lugo's wife reminds him that she bought his shirt at Sogo, the local Japanese department store. He haughtily takes it off and throw it away with glee. Beaming with excitement and crassly eyeing the bosoms of other female protesters, Lugo seizes the opportunity and cheers, "Those who are wearing Japanese underwear, throw them away!" Somewhat caught off guard by Lugo's fervor, his wife whispers to him and asks if she should take hers off too. Lugo hovers over her, as if to protect her from other prying eyes, and sheepishly utters, "No need for that, no need for that."

Bodyguards of the Last Governor belongs to the Hong Kong cinema genre that is replete with crass inside jokes, political satire, and local references. The anti-Japanese scene described above, however, poignantly reveals the duality of "Japan" in postwar East Asia: Japan as former military violence and Japan as postwar economic and cultural desire. References to militarism and the disputed islands point to the unresolved historical trauma suffered by the Chinese people at the hands of the Japanese imperialists. The cry to boycott Japanese goods refers to the economic and cultural expansionism of postwar Japan in the region and beyond. The waves of anti-Japan banners allow the protesters (and film spectators) to easily draw a single line connecting Japan's prewar political imperialism with its postwar new imperialism. However, the diegesis of the scenes described above refuses this facile and nationalistic reading of anti-imperialism. The references to sushi and Japan-made underwear, not to mention other Japanese commodities not featured in the film, only accentuate the pervasiveness of Japanese cultural penetration (as with other globalizing forces) into the lives and onto the bodies of the Hong Kongers, even as they fiercely protest against Japan.

The disjuncture between political demand and cultural acceptance in the film's anti-Japan sequence renders visible the definitive form of anti-Japanism in postwar Asia: it is a paradox that defies simple definition and that is simultaneously about and not about "Japan." The protest tells us less about the actually existing "Japan" than the context of "Hong Kong" in which anti-Japanism conjures certain desire and fantasy about the putative notion of Japan. In its most direct form, anti-Japanism is a criticism of Japan's imperialist legacy and its reluctance to come to terms with that past and to accept its responsibilities with sincere apologies and proper redress. In its rallying and allegorical capacity to take Japan as an object of derision, anti-Japanism reveals much about domestic conditions in places such as Hong Kong, South Korea, or China. The film, after all, is a satirical displacement of the anxiety over the 1997 handover, and the anti-Japan scene can be interpreted as a mocking of the fickleness of political commitments among the Hong Kongers. But we must also ask: why do social anxieties and political concerns in postcolonial East Asia take the form of anti-Japanism? As I will argue here, anti-Japanism in East Asia is a symptom of unsettled historical trauma of the Japanese empire and its legacy. Or, in short, it is the failure of decolonization, on the one hand and, on the other hand, also a manifestation of the changing geopolitical configuration of the region under the demands and strains of global capitalism. The unilateral dominance of Japan in the region since the Meiji period is giving ways to more multilateral, and more contentious, relations to other East Asian nations, especially in the context of the rise of China.

Anti-Japanism in East Asia

At a talk given at Duke University on book banning, the famed author Yan Lianke made a humorous remark on the absurdity of censorship in contemporary China. According to Yan, despite the plethora of conflicts with foreigners in modern Chinese history—the British come to mind immediately, but also Russians and Americans—only one such conflict, the Second Sino-Japanese War (1937–45), is allowed, and even encouraged, to be produced for public consumption in Chinese media, especially around the National Day. These anti-Japanese shows are so prevalent that Yan and his friends often joked that the number of Japanese characters killed in one year in Chinese films and TV dramas would amount to the entire population of Japan (127 million)! Yan has, however, seriously underestimated the number of Japanese casualties: of the two hundred or so TV dramas aired during prime time on all Chinese satellite channels in 2012, seventy were about the Second Sino-Japanese wars or spy wars. In Hengdian World Studio, the largest film studio in Asia, located in Zhejiang province, it is estimated that seven hundred million "Japanese soldiers" died at the hands of Chinese patriots that year alone![1]

Anti-Japanism is neither new nor exclusive to East Asia. In the United States, for instance, there has been a long history of anti-Japan movements: immigration exclusion acts in the early 1900s, internment camps of Japanese Americans and anti-Japan mobilization during the Second World War, and Japan bashing in the 1980s. What is arguably common among all anti-Japanism in the United States is the fear of the Other manifested through racism, be it the threat of Japan as a competing imperialist power (after the Russo-Japanese War) or as an economic rival (after the Plaza Accord). For the United States, and perhaps for Europe as well, anti-Japanism arises when "Western" hegemony is threatened by the real or perceived rise of Japan, a non-Western, nonwhite empire. Anti-Japanism in East Asia requires a different interpretation and historicization than that of the United States although racism within Asia is growing amid mounting political tensions.

To begin, we need to distinguish at least two forms of anti-Japanism: "resist-Japan" (抗日) and "anti-Japan" (反日) in East Asia. "Resist Japan" is widely used in mainland China and the Sinophone world to convey the efforts and success of Chinese struggle against Japanese imperialism, especially during the eight-year "war of resistance" (1937–45). "Anti-Japanism" is a decidedly postwar phenomenon that saw its emergence in the immediate postwar years. Anti-Japanism was mobilized in newly "liberated" former colonies, such as Korea and Taiwan, for the building of political power to unify the "nation."[2] With the end of the Korean War and the consolidation of the Cold War structure in East Asia, anti-Japanism was soon replaced by anti-Communism and the imposition of martial laws in both countries. In the early 1970s, concomitant with Japanese economic expansionism into Southeast Asia and America's decision to "return" the Senkaku/Diaoyu islands to Japan as part of the Ryūkyū/Okinawa reversion in 1972, anti-Japanese movements erupted in the region: the Malari Incident of 1974 and the Protest Diaoyu Island movements, for example.[3] Anti-Japanism in the 1970s was a diasporic and transpacific movement led mainly by students from Hong Kong and Taiwan in the United States (Wang 2013). Anti-Japanism took on the form of a Chinese cultural nationalism with Bruce Lee as its filmic symbolic icon (see chapter 1). China, ironically, was not part of the first wave of postwar anti-Japanese movements. Lee's films were banned from mainland China until the 1980s. The Communist regime was insisting on building bilateral relations with the Japanese as the two nations reestablished diplomatic relations in 1972. The early 1970s also saw the dissipation of the postwar 1960s antisecurity treaty and peace movement in Japan and coincided with Japan's growing confidence and reentrance into the capitalist market without opposition in the region. It is therefore not a coincidence that Jon Halliday and Gavan McCormack's *Japanese Imperialism Today: "Co-prosperity in Greater East Asia,"* was published in 1974, signaling a "return" of Japanese capital to its former empire as it shifted its lower-end manufacturing facilities to other developing nations in Asia.

Anti-Japanism gained momentum in the early 1980s with an economically confident Japan attempting to revise history textbooks by whitewashing its imperialist aggressions. In August 1991, Kim Hak-Soon, a former "comfort woman," publicly testified about her experience as a sexual slave under the Japanese military during the Second World War and filed a lawsuit against the Japanese government. Her "coming out" radically challenged the masculinist, patriarchal, and nationalist suppression and denial of sexual violence between the Korean and Japanese governments in the postwar years. Amid the Japanese government's continued eschewal and abrogation, weekly Wednesday protests by former comfort women and their supporters are, to this day, held in front of the Japanese embassy in Seoul.

Another contentious issue that elicits strong anti-Japanese sentiments is memories and contention over the Nanking Massacre. The atrocity was tacitly acknowledged but strategically suppressed by the postwar governments of China, Japan, and the United States. It was not until the publications of *Travels in China* (1972) by the Japanese journalist Honda Katsuichi, and *The Rape of Nanking* (1997) by the Chinese-American writer Iris Chang, that this historical event became politicized, especially in the 2000s with Japanese neoconservatives' repudiation and Chinese insistence on their own victimization (Yoshida 2006).

In 2005, massive protests against Japan erupted throughout major cities in China. The protesters cited the Japanese government's ambition to join the UN Security Council and former prime minister Koizumi Jun'ichirō's continued visit to the Yasukuni Shrine that deified the Japanese war dead (and subjects of Japanese empire) as signs of a lack of remorse and reflection on the history of Japanese aggression as reasons for their outrage. Tensions between China and Japan have since continued unabated, as witnessed by the more violent Chinese protests in 2012 and by China's own ambition to establish hegemony, including territorial claims that extend beyond East Asia to Southeast Asia. The cursory and selective account is to situate anti-Japanism within its historical conditions of possibility and its pattern of emergence, eruption and ebbing since the 1970s. It is also important to differentiate popular and official anti-Japanism although they are imbricated and implicated in ways that are difficult to separate completely. The comfort women's demand for redress and reparation, based on years of denial and shaming, is qualitatively different from the Korean state's own suppression and instrumental usage of anti-Japanism for its political gains, for example. However, the Korean government has no qualms about appropriating the plight of the comfort women for its political tussle with Japan. Similarly, the comfort women and their supporters often resort to nationalist discourse for their confrontation with the Japanese state.

As mentioned above, it is important to differentiate the various phrases used to describe both adverse and favorable feelings toward Japan. The range of these vocabularies not only differentiates Asian sentiments toward Japan from the West, but also charts the shifting nuances of "Japan" in Asia from empire to Cool Japan. Besides "resist Japan" and "anti-Japan" (mentioned earlier), there is "hate Japan" (仇日), which is used to describe the hatred for Japan as a sickness, an extreme condition of hostility, like an archenemy. Then there's something like "repel Japan" (排日), which is mostly used during legal contexts of exclusion of Japanese immigration. Anti-Japanism has its constitutive Other in pro-Japanism or sentiments favoring Japan. This seemingly oppositional pair are interdependent and in fact share a similar fantasy or desire about some ideas of "Japan." "Pro-Japan" (親日) has the sense of being intimate with Japan and is usually used by anti-Japanese nationalists when condemning those who collaborated with Japanese rule and who, by definition, betrayed the nation. This is particularly sensitive and incriminating in the postcolonial Korean context, where the *chinilpai*, or factions that collaborated with Japanese rule, are still being prosecuted today (Kwon 2015). In the Chinese context, those who conspired with the Japanese imperialists are simply called "betrayer of the Han race" (漢奸) or "running dogs" (走狗), signifying the centrality of the Chinese race and reducing abettors to subhumans. "Worship Japan" (崇日) denotes Japanophiles who harbor sentiments of reverence toward Japan, usually disparagingly referring to the Taiwanese preference for Japan over mainland China. In recent years, two terms, "loving Japan" (哈日) and "deep affection for Japan" (萌日), are deployed to characterize younger generations' preference and addiction for Japanese popular culture in Taiwan and mainland China, respectively. What is significant in the new generations' infatuation with Japanese popular culture is not only that it provides another option of consumption from American-dominant pop culture under global capitalism, but also that it signifies the increasing co-evalness among Asian youth and creating a transnational community of fandom that has the potential to transcend the parochialism and nationalism marred by previous generations' personal and secondary experience of Japanese colonialism and imperialism.

Bodyguards of the Last Governor's parodic juxtaposition of "Japan" as both violence and desire is akin to what Yoshimi Shun'ya has argued about the presence of "America" in postwar Japan and Asia (Yoshimi and Buist 2003). Analyzing "America" from a region-wide context (but mainly focusing on Japan) from the perspective of people's everyday consciousness, Yoshimi makes two important observations regarding postwar geopolitics in Asia: first, that the United States has displaced, replaced, and subsumed the Japanese empire in the region in the Cold War era. The American Occupation and policymakers have collaborated with the conservative Japanese government in making Japan the "economic" hub of Asia, reversing its original plan of radical demilitarization and democratization. Second, the geopolitical calculus of rehabilitating Japan as an economic pivot in the transpacific alliance—as part of a project to construct an anti-Communist bloc—created a division of labor among the Asian nations. Okinawa, Taiwan, South Korea, and the Philippines bear the burden of large American military functions and installations. Meanwhile mainland Japan concentrated on economic development. As a result, according to Yoshimi, two "Americas" began to emerge on mainland Japan in the late 1950s: the America of violence, mainly surrounding military installations; and the America of desire, a model of middle-class lifestyle and consumption (Yoshimi and Buist 2003: 439). In postwar Asia and Japan, Yoshimi argues, "America" prohibits, seduces, and fragments. Hence, anti-Americanism and pro-Americanism are not binary oppositions but are intertwined, interdependent and intersecting in complicated and, at times, contradictory ways.

The "embrace" between America and Japan assured that America would be the sole inheritor of the Japanese empire. American postwar hegemony is a reconstruction of the Japanese empire that existed until the end of the war. The transfiguration of Japanese imperial order from wartime to postwar under America's watch not only exonerated American violence during the war, but also obfuscated Japanese imperialism and colonialism in Asia. The symbol of this mutual "conditional forgiveness," to borrow the phrase from Jacques Derrida (2001), is none other than the cenotaph erected at the Hiroshima Peace Memorial, which reads "Please rest in peace, for the error shall not be repeated." As Oda Makoto and others have argued, the ambiguity of the subject in the Japanese language does not specify who is responsible for the "error" (Tanaka 2007). Furthermore, if it was the Japanese, then they are compelled to apologize for a crime they did not commit, consequently absolving America's crime of dropping the bombs. More symbolically for the Japanese empire in Asia, the Peace Center and the Memorial Park were commissioned to Tange Kenzō, who also designed the Commemorative Building Project for the Construction of Greater East Asia in 1942. The project was supposed to monumentalize the notorious concept of the Greater East Asian Co-Prosperity Sphere, the Japanese imperialist vision of regional unity to counter the West. The stylistic origin of the Memorial Park can be traced back to almost an identical ground plan for the Commemorative Building Project (Starrs 2001: 173). The connection and transformation between wartime and postwar can also be discerned in the construction of the Nagasaki Peace Park. The *heiwa-kinen-zō*, or peace statue, a massive masculine figure, was commissioned to a local sculptor, Kitamura Seibō, and completed in 1955. Kitamura was a member of the Imperial Art Association during the Asia/Pacific war. He had produced statues of military figures, and all were muscled, large, and combative. For example, he created the statue of Terauchi Misatake, who was instrumental in the annexation of the Korean Peninsula in 1910. The selection of Kitamura's peace statue represents somewhat of a comeback of not only Kitamura's career, but also his insistence of producing masculine military figures (now rearticulated as pacifism). Many of Kitamura's wartime statues were either torn down, removed, or replaced by "feminine" figures that represent postwar pacifism (Otsuki 2016: 409). The Nagasaki Peace Statue then can be read as the recuperation of masculinity in postwar Japan as peace and democracy rather than war and militarism.

The transition, from empire to subimperialism, is not a continuation of the same, but is a reconfiguration of imperial and wartime militarism to postwar pacifism and democracy. In short, war defeat replaced decolonization (or deimperialization in Chen Kuan-Hsing's usage [2010]) and the possibility of postcolonial reflexivity. It is in this postwar Cold War context of American hegemony and a Japanese failure of deimperialization that framed and hence inhibited the process of decolonization in the former Japanese empire. Unlike French or British where decolonization often accompanied violent struggles for independence, the end of the Japanese empire was a result of war defeat and was followed by the Cold War. If, in Japan, democracy and demilitarization replaced or hijacked the process of deimperialization, in the former colonies, postwar settlement and nationalist recuperation replaced decolonization as a radical political and cultural process. The lack of deimperialization of Japan and the decolonization of Japan's former empire sowed the seeds of anti-Japanism in Asia that began to sprout in the early 1970s and continue to grow to this day. It is in the context of the Cold War suspension or obfuscation that Chen Kuan-Hsing calls for the simultaneous processes of deimperialization (for the former colonizer), decolonization (for the former colonized) and de–Cold War (for everyone) in East Asia and beyond (2010).

Asia's Anti-Japanism and Japan's Anti-Americanism

Anti-Japanism finds its corollary in ethnonationalism. In this regard, anti-Japanism produces similar effects both outside and inside Japan in fanning nationalistic sentiments and operating through the binary discourse of "us" and "them." Just like Japan's anti-Americanism, Asia's anti-Japanism, for the neoconservatives, is closely linked to nationalism and cultural solipsism. For the Japanese neoconservatives, anti-Americanism and anti-Japanism converge on the ways Japan was deformed and disfigured by its forcible transformation into a client status, inaugurating what has come to be known as the "long postwar" that the Japanese have been living since 1945. As a result, they seek to revitalize "Japanism" to counter Americanism and Asia's anti-Japanism. Yamano Sharin, the author of the infamous manga *Kenkanryū* (Hating the Korean wave) (2005), calls anti-Japanism a "sickness." Nishimura Kohyu, the journalist, considers anti-Japanism a "magma" that is erupting. Nishimura argues in *The Structure of Anti-Japan* (2012) that, in order for the Japanese to overcome "anti-Japanism," they must begin by searching for the identity of Japan and the Japanese (17). This is to be done, according to Nishimura, by returning to history, culture, and tradition from a "linear" perspective. The reason that the Japanese do not possess a linear sense of history, he argues, is because of its war defeat and has been "ruled by the historical perspective that the past was evil" (19). The culprit of this truncated conceptualization of history is the American Occupation and those Japanese who embraced defeat and complied with policies from the Supreme Commander of the Allied Powers. Seven years and eight months of the occupation created a "blank of history" that severed historical continuity between the pre- and postwar generations. Nishimura then presses for the return of "autonomy" to Japan. He cites John Dower and Herbert Bix's books as a continuation of American hegemony over Japan (20).[4]

After identifying the American Occupation as being responsible for Japan's "nonlinear" historical consciousness, Nishimura turns to Asia and anti-Japanism. He places the "prototype" of anti-Japanism in 1982 when Chinese and Koreans protested against Japan's textbook revisions. He sees the "structure of anti-Japanism" forming at this moment when Japanese leftists and media colluded with Asian nationalists in criticizing Japan (23). It is noteworthy that Nishimura uses the word "prototype" with anti-Japanism and locates its emergence only in the early 1980s. As I discussed above, one can trace the emergence of anti-Japanism in postwar East Asia as early as 1948 and definitely by the early 1970s. Nishimura seems to have developed a similar historical amnesia that he accuses others of having. Nishimura argues that anti-Japanism is endangering the Japanese identity that linked the Japanese people to the emperor and the imperial family (26). Along with the Greater East Asian War and the Nanjing Incident (his phrase), Nishimura cites the criticism of the imperial household as one of the attempts by the Chinese and Japanese leftists to destroy Japanese "memory." For neoconservatives like Nishimura and others, anti-Japanism is an extension, if not an amplification, of Americanism that severs Japan from its history, culture, and the imperial system. Instead of embracing anti-Japanism in a self-reflexive way, the anger of the Asian neighbors simply rekindles the desire to reestablish Japan as a "normal" nation freed from its "masochist" view of history. To this extent, anti-Japanism becomes an alibi, an opportunity, to voice the conservatives' long-standing anti-Americanism. Anti-Japanism and anti-Americanism coalesce in the form of reconstituting Japanism.

Anti-Japanism, Anti-Americanism, and Post–East Asia

The 2005 anti-Japan demonstration in China prompted many in Japan to ask a similar question in the immediate aftermath of 9/11 in the United States: "Why do they hate us?" The question in itself is innocent enough. Yet it belies its simplicity as a rhetoric of feigned denial. The question works like a floating signifier, whereby different and competing answers or perspectives can be posited, debated, redefined, and related, depending on one's political persuasion and worldview. Furthermore, the question also assumes a binary between a purported incommensurable "they" and "us" and the irreconcilable self-definition and foreign (mis)perception.

The images of the 2005 spring protests shocked the Japanese public in two ways. First, there was a general disbelief that Japan and the Japanese could be so despised by others. The issues of Japanese invasion and war responsibilities did not often sink in immediately. Rather, they appeared anachronistic, as if belonging to another era to another people. Second, people were bewildered at the modern cityscapes and rapid development seen on the news, which were utterly unthinkable due to the conventional image of China as backward and underdeveloped. In short, there was a gap between seeing and believing. As Mizoguchi Yūzō (2005) has pointed out, this disjuncture or gap between the actually existing China and Japan's idea of China points to the historical fact that Japan does not have a shared experience with the global south and that Japan's conceptualization of Asia, which is vital in its modern/colonial self-definition, is utterly out of date. Mizoguchi periodizes two moments of modernity: the first half from 1850 to 1950, and the second half from 1950 to 2050. There might be some problem with this periodization, but Mizoguchi's point is that Japan's conceptualization of Asia remains in that of the first half of modernity while the real Asia is far along toward the second half of modernity. In short, anti-Japanism points to the limit of modern Japanese thought on Asia. The modern/colonial framework that enabled Japan's self-identity vis-à-vis the West and Asia is no longer feasible in grasping the fast-changing condition of globality. For the East Asian left, anti-Japanism also rekindles the question of Americanism. For scholars like Chen Kuan-Hsing, Sun Ge, and Baik Youngseo (2006), a "post–East Asia" world is only possible with the end of the American military presence as its premise. Inter-referencing among Asian peoples, or what Chen calls Asia as method, requires the de-Americanization in the region since the conceptualization of East Asia is itself an American invention in the Cold War period, as we have seen earlier. If modern/colonial East Asia is constituted primarily through Japanese imperialism and American neocolonialism, linking anti-Japanism and anti-Americanism might enable us to radically reconfigure and reconceptualize the region beyond the Japanese and American imaginary.

The Form of Anti-Japanism (and Pro-Japanism)

I want to suggest that anti-Japanism consists of at least four distinctive but interrelated sets of attributes: (1) a set of competing claims and narratives about Japan or, more precisely, the "idea" of Japan; (2) a set of performative acts and representations; (3) a set of emotions and sentiments; and (4) a set of temporary fixes to political, economic, and social crises. First, anti-Japanism is an exaggerated version of ideas, traits, and postures about Japan that are believed to be quite distinct from those of other cultures or countries. From "Japanese devils" to "economic animals," negative images of Japan are first conjured as violating national sovereignty and sanctity. The claims can range from Japan's refusal to come to terms with its imperialist past to Japan's economic influence over domestic markets. Pro-Japanese sentiments also share similar, albeit favorable, hyperbolic representations of Japan. This does not mean that these claims are false or nonexistent, but that they are amplified, partial truths.[5]

Second, anti-Japanism operates on a collective level and is inherently social. Anti-Japanism often enacts itself in the form of public demonstration with slogans, posters, and flyers, with numbers that range from hundreds as in the Wednesdays demonstration in South Korea, to thousands, like in major cities in China in 2005 and 2012. What is important about the demonstrations is that they are demonstrative: they elicit certain visual representations that can be disseminated, circulated, and reproduced.

Third, anti-Japanism (and pro-Japanism) cannot substantiate itself without sentiments. Or, rather, sentiments can make anti-Japanism sustainable and produce collective catharsis. These feelings (experiential), emotions (social), and affects (unconscious and corporeal) all make the externalization of anti-Japanism possible. These sentiments, however, are not uniform or consistent. They are highly dependent on personal histories, collective memories, and contingencies of the protest milieu.

Finally, anti-Japanism ultimately reflects more on the anxieties and desires of the protesting society than on Japan itself. It is, in the final analysis, a displacement of social unease caused by political and economic upheavals. It represents temporary fixes to domestic political crises by projecting Japan in various forms, from threat to foe, from ally to refuge. That said, we must ask why this projection or deferral takes the form of anti-Japanism and not something else.

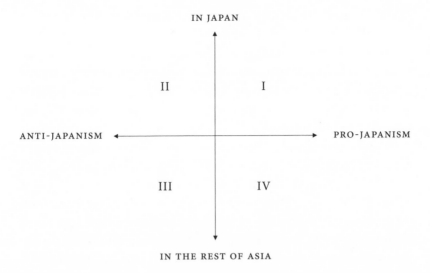

II   I

ANTI-JAPANISM ←————————————→ PRO-JAPANISM

III   IV

IN THE REST OF ASIA

Anti-Japanism and its constitutive other, pro-Japanism, in East Asia is represented in the figure above, with each quadrant representing a range of possible positions. The figure is intended to convey the range of emotions and geopolitical positions between Japan and Asia. Quadrant I consists of moderate to neoconservative positions in Japan; quadrant II includes leftists and the internationalist critique of Japanese imperialism; quadrant III comprises various nationalist and anti-Japanese elements in China, the Koreas, and Taiwan; and finally, quadrant IV represents positions favorable to Japan, from the formerly colonized to contemporary youths obsessed with Japanese popular culture. The figure and its respective quadrants depict multiple relations that, due to historical and local conditions, cannot be easily collapsed into homogeneous pro- or anti-Japan sentiments. For example, colonial difference—the incommensurability between the colonizer and the colonized—signals different desires between the Japanese conservatives (quadrant I) and the Taiwanese imperial subjects (quadrant IV) although they share similar pro-Japan sentiments. I discuss this specifically in chapter 4.

It is important to note that, like any discursive formation, anti-Japanism is not static. While anti-Japanism in postwar Asia mostly takes on the *form* of demands for apologies and atonements for colonial wounds or war crimes (colonialism and imperialism), the *content* is often directed at local and present concerns that may or may not have anything to do with Japan. The degree of intensity of anti-Japanism is conditioned by the relative power relationship between Japan and other nations in the world system. Furthermore, the *range* of anti-Japanism spans several scales. From personal memories of Japanese atrocities to collective demands for redress and reparation, from the casual slur of "Japanese devils" to an official discourse of condemnation, anti-Japanism stirs feelings and emotions—anger, sadness, envy, and so on—that are intense, mixed, and at times contradictory.

In his thoughtful analysis of post–Cold War American hegemony, Chris Connery argues for the "continued necessity of anti-Americanism" today because, "in certain forms, anti-Americanism can be a key component of a powerful and effective anti-capitalist politics, and can preserve necessary and important spaces of counter-hegemony and critique" (2001: 400). Anti-Americanism, however, frequently and invariably takes the nation-state as its primary platform. And as Karatani Kōjin (2014) has argued, capital, nation, and the state form a Borromean knot, reinforcing and supplementing one another, depending on the crises and needs of capitalism. As a consequence, globalization would not entail the end of the nation or the state, as some have hoped. Instead, it only creates conditions for their rearticulations. In this regard, because global capitalism is a social relation and the ruling classes of all capitalist nation-states have a stake in the reproduction of capitalist social relations, Connery cautions that any anti-Americanism that strengthens the nation-state will be a double-edged sword. Nation-based and state-sanctioned anti-Americanism becomes dangerous and politically regressive when it is explicit in constructing the nation-state itself as an alternative social collectivity (403). Despite these shortcomings, Connery views anti-Americanism as having "an important structural capacity to link the energy of the negative to the sphere of global ideological reproduction" (403). Anti-Japanism in East Asia must be apprehended as this double-edged sword as well.

Not all anti-Japanism confers the same political desire or represents similar grievances against Japan. Anti-Japanism enacted by the former comfort women occupies very different structural and power relations to the Japanese state as compared to anti-Japanism fanned by the Chinese state to displace its citizens' growing anxiety over precariousness and social unrest. Ethnonationalism and anti-Japanism work in complicity to prevent genuine exchange and reconciliation over historical issues and contemporary problems afflicting peoples in the region. Connery hopes anti-Americanism (despite his reservations mentioned above) can produce progressive social collectives against the universal nation-state that is the United States. I see anti-Japanism as less a panacea to Japanese capitalism or regional reconciliation. Instead, I argue that anti-Japanism (and pro-Japanism) represents a shifting of power relations in East Asia in the post–Cold War era. The rise of China has radically transformed the U.S.-Japan dominance of the region since the end of the Second World War. How to imagine an anti-Japanism (and its negative power) without falling into the trap of ethnonationalism remains a formidable challenge.

Chapter Outline

The book is organized around the theme of anti-Japanism (and pro-Japanism, its constitutive Other) in three East Asian spaces: mainland China, South Korea, and Taiwan, with an emphasis on cultural representations, with "postcoloniality" and "sentimentality" as unifying concepts. Unlike the falls of the French and British empires, which were due to independence movements in their colonies, the dissolution of the formal Japanese empire occurred primarily through its war defeat. This particular demise of the empire has had two consequences that contributed to the failure of decolonization. First, for the Japanese, the overwhelming defeat at the hands of Americans, especially the dropping of the two bombs and subsequent occupation, contributed to the perception that Japan lost the war to the Americans and not to the Chinese. Furthermore, war defeat and postwar demilitarization conflated, if not replaced, questions of empire and decolonization. In relation to Taiwan, Japan's defeat was appropriated by the nationalist government to contrast the heroic endeavors of the "liberating" regime and the "slave" mentality of the colonial Taiwanese, thus justifying the nationalist recolonization of the island. After four years of civil war ending in the Communist victory, the nationalist government relocated to Taiwan and the two regimes have been mired in the Cold War structure that continued, albeit in different form, to this day. The situation on the Korean Peninsula was similar. Independence was soon followed by a division into North and South Korea, the North propped up by the Communist Soviet Union and the South by the capitalist United States, which suited the exigencies of the emerging Cold War. The devastating Korean War further entrenched the divided system even in the so-called post–Cold War era. However, as I argue in chapter 4, the repression by the nationalist government in post-1949 Taiwan and subsequent democratization prompted a "nostalgia" for an imagined Japan, a nostalgia that likely contributed to the stereotypical opposition between anti-Japanese Koreans and pro-Japanese Taiwanese. It is to address the failed decolonization within the not-yet-over Cold War that Chen Kuan-Hsing proposes decolonialization, deimperialization and de–Cold War as a three-pronged method to rethink and reengage Asia. My analysis and critique of anti-Japanism join Chen's call for confronting the lack of decolonization in the Japanese empire and for reimagining a post–East Asia unencumbered by Cold War divisions and colonial legacies.

Naoki Sakai and others (2005) have argued that the myth of the mono-ethnic society cannot be debunked with merely empirical attempts to illuminate its truth or falsity. More importantly, Sakai recognizes that the "sense of being Japanese cannot be analyzed according to a methodology of the history of ideas, but rather functions through the emotional dimension" (3). It is this "sentiment of nationality"—the regime of representations of community constituted through the apparatuses of fantasies and imaginations within the modern national community—that undergirds and animates the emotions, feelings, and passions of national competition and divisions in the world today. My study, set within the context of anti-Japanese sentimentality in postwar postcolonial East Asia, comprises ways to analyze the "regime of fantasies and imaginations," which Sakai sees as an important affective dimension of the modern national community. For example, I contrast the dominant (and masculine and culturalist) emotion of *han* (an unresolved resentment against injustice) with the notion of "shame" felt by the so-called military comfort women in South Korea. I argue that "shame," or rather the overcoming of feelings of shame, offers a possible reconciliation for some comfort women, not with the Japanese state but with loved ones. Feelings of national "humiliation," I argue, have animated Chinese anti-Japanism since the late 1980s. I trace the shifting meanings of the term "Japanese devils" as a trope to reflect on China's own self-definition. In the case of Taiwan, I suggest that the sentiments of "sadness" and "nostalgia" dominate many elderly Taiwanese feelings for an imagined "Japan." This nostalgia, I argue, has less to do with Japan than with resentment toward the neocolonialism of the Kuomintang regime in postwar Taiwan. These sentimentalities—*han*, shame, humiliation, nostalgia—form the collective and differentiated affects conditioned by the shifting geopolitical terrains in postwar postcolonial East Asia in the wake of Japanese imperialism and colonialism. Finally, it is to continue the line of argument of sentimentality that I attempt to articulate the political concept of "love" and intergenerational intimacy in the hope of imagining a transnational and subnational politics of affect in the conclusion.

Chapter 1, "When Bruce Lee Meets Gojira: Transimperial Characters, Anti-Japanism, Anti-Americanism, and the Failure of Decolonization," argues that the symbolic anti-Americanism of *Gojira* (1954) and the anti-Japanism of Bruce Lee's *Fist of Fury* (1974) constitute two axes of desire and fantasy that characterize the failure of decolonization in postwar East Asia. The sudden disappearance of the Japanese empire after Japan's defeat, the subsequent American hegemony in the region during the Cold War, combined with entrenched authoritarian rule in former colonies, such as Taiwan and South Korea, and, finally, Japan's postwar economic ascendancy all contributed to the suspension, if not outright repression, of legacies of the Japanese empire. It is only in the so-called post–Cold War era (and, in the case of China, the postsocialist era) that issues of Japanese empire—war responsibilities, territorial disputes, comfort women, the Yasukuni Shrine, and so forth—became contentious in the region's public spheres.

Chapter 2, "'Japanese Devils': The Conditions and Limits of Anti-Japanism in China," analyzes one instance of modern Sino-Japanese relations: the epithet "riben guizi," or Japanese devils, in Chinese popular culture. I locate the representation of Japanese devils in four historical moments: late Sinocentric imperium, high imperialism, socialist nationalism, and postsocialist globalization. I suggest that while this "hate word" performs an affective politics of recognition stemming from an ineluctable trauma of imperialist violence, it ultimately fails to establish a politics of reconciliation. I argue that anti-Japanism in China is less about Japan itself than about China's own self-image, mediated through its asymmetrical power relations with Japan throughout its modern history.

Chapter 3, "Shameful Bodies, Bodily Shame: 'Comfort Women' and Anti-Japanism in South Korea," turns to the sentiment of shame regarding sexual violence. I analyze Byun Young-Joo's trilogy about the comfort women through the affect of shame and the trope of the body. Unlike the culturalist sentiment of *han* in Korean nationalist discourse, shame, or rather the overcoming of shame, has the potential to negotiate and move forward the politics of reconciliation. If shame constitutes the affective dimension of these women's existence, the aging body reminds us of the materiality of their suffering and the inevitable passage of time that further underscores the cruelty of "postcolonial" violence. Juxtaposing and associating the visibly aged women's bodies with that of Emperor Hirohito's dying and concealed body and the nationalized mourning surrounding his death, I argue not only that the bodies are differentially valued and evaluated, but also that the cowardice of the imperial system once again abrogated the responsibility of the Showa emperor for Japanese imperialism and colonialism.

Unlike earlier chapters on anti-Japanism, chapter 4, "Colonial Nostalgia or Postcolonial Anxiety: The *Dōsan* Generation In-Between 'Retrocession' and 'Defeat,'" explores the sentiment of nostalgia and intimacy toward Japanese colonialism, as displayed by former colonial subjects in Taiwan. I argue that the favorable and at times intense feelings toward "Japan"—imagined or real—must be seen as a desire to recuperate a sense of loss in both personal and historical terms. I understand their passion as a belated plea for recognition from the former colonizers of their marginalized existence since the end of formal colonialism. Their efforts, despite the obvious pro-Japan sentiments, interrupt two linear narratives of (1) colonialism → retrocession → nation-building and (2) colonialism → war defeat → nation-building schematics espoused and expounded by the Kuomintang government and by the Japanese state, respectively.

In chapter 5, "'In the Name of Love': Critical Regionalism and Co-Viviality in Post–East Asia," I examine four representations of love, or instantiations of the *political concept* of love, in postwar postcolonial East Asia (in *Gojira* [1954], *Death by Hanging* [1968], *Mohist Attack* [1992–96], and *My Own Breathing* [1999]) that offer glimpses of possibility for transnational and subnational intimacies and affective belonging that transcend love of the nation and love of the same. Finally, using Taiwan and its seemingly pro-Japanese sentiments and its marginalization in East Asian geopolitics, I argue for a reconceptualization of the politics of reconciliation. In chapter 6, "Reconciliation Otherwise: Intimacy, Indigeneity, and the Taiwan Difference," I read contrapuntally Tsushima Yūko's novel *Exceedingly Barbaric* (2008) with Laha Mebow's documentary film *Finding Sayun* (2010), and I argue for an intergenerational reconciliation that displaces both the colonial narrative and state-centric politics of compromise and settlement.

ONE. When Bruce Lee Meets Gojira: Transimperial
Characters, Anti-Japanism, Anti-Americanism,
and the Failure of Decolonization

As far as I know, the famed martial artist never fought the scaly monster. Neither has the nuclear-infected beast stomped and destroyed the homeland of the fictionalized Chinese patriot. Their closest encounter appears briefly in the World Martial Arts Tournament in the episode "Milk Delivery" in *Dragon Ball*, the popular Japanese manga and anime series. In the brief combat scene, Bruce Lee at first easily defeats what appears to be a giant gorilla (an obvious King Kong reference) with a high kick and his trademark high-pitched screech. However, he is soon charred by Gojira's signature radioactive flames.[1] The fictive battle in this popular animation series underscores the continued reference to, and relevance of, the two "global icons" in popular culture, each outliving their respective life spans (the original *Gojira* opened in theaters in 1954 and the series purportedly ended in 2004 with *Gojira: Final Wars*; Bruce Lee, born on November 27, 1940, died July 20, 1973).[2] These global icons, however, have their own local and regional histories and itineraries. While Gojira made its transpacific journey to become Godzilla in the United States in 1956, Bruce Lee made the opposite trek to Asia and then back to the United States with his last full-featured film, *Enter the Dragon*, in 1973. In this regard, America looms large in the popular receptions of these cinematic icons.

The global popularity of Gojira and Bruce Lee notwithstanding, I want to focus on their more limited historical conjuncture—specifically Japan, Asia, and the United States. I want to suggest that the historical condition of possibilities for Gojira and Bruce Lee reside in the "postwar Cold

War system" where "postcoloniality" in the Asia-Pacific region remains unresolved and repressed, yet contested.[3] More precisely, I want to argue that the "symbolic anti-Americanism" of *Gojira* and the "anti-Japanism" of Bruce Lee's *Fist of Fury* (1974) constitute two axes of desire and fantasy that characterize the "failure of decolonization" in postwar East Asia. The sudden disappearance of the Japanese empire after Japan's defeat, the subsequent American hegemony in the region during the Cold War, combined with entrenched authoritarian rule in former colonies such as Taiwan and South Korea, and finally Japan's postwar economic ascendancy all contributed to the suspension, if not outright repression, of legacies of the Japanese empire. It is only in the so-called post–Cold War era (and, in the case of China, postsocialist era) that issues of Japanese empire—war responsibilities, territorial disputes, "comfort women," the Yasukuni Shrine, and so on—became contentious in the region's public sphere. Here (as with the "post" in "postcolonial") "post–Cold War" in East Asia does not signal the end of the Cold War. The Taiwan Strait, the Korean Peninsula, and Okinawa are still mired in a Cold War framework, despite the end of East-West conflict in other parts of the world. If the older Cold War structure is visible through the lens of socialist/capitalist conflict, the current post–Cold War structure is almost completely subsumed under global capitalism despite official North Korean and Chinese claims that socialism is the dominant state ideology. In short, what we have in the region today is the coexistence of political Cold War structure and economic neoliberal globalization with popular culture comprising a diverse and contradictory variation between the two.

As products of Cold War anxieties, Gojira and Bruce Lee are therefore not just global icons, but what I call "transimperial characters" that attempt to cope with the trauma of Japan's defeat and the history of Chinese humiliation in the modern colonial world. Transimperial refers to the transition, transfer, translation, and transposition of imperial regimes, in this case, the shift from the Japanese to the American empire and their overlapping (and colluding) operation and extension of global capitalism in the region. Gojira and Bruce Lee are "characters" in the sense that they mediate between the fantasy (2-D) and real (3-D) worlds (Nozawa 2013). As semiotic mediations, Gojira enacts a symbolic anti-Americanism that tacitly criticizes the United States for its nuclear activities and expresses Japan's own inability to reconcile the contradiction between its war dead and its Asian victims. Bruce Lee's films, especially *Fist of Fury*, dramatize a symbolic anti-imperialism that heals the colonial wound through an abstract Chinese cultural nationalism that, ironically, has nothing to do with mainland China.

Gojira's repeated return to Tokyo and Bruce Lee's revenge against his Japanese foes represent two sides of the same postcolonial coin: Japan's war defeat and the abrupt dissolution of the empire on the one hand and the memories of Japanese imperialism/colonialism that remain contentious and unresolved to this day on the other. Gojira's footsteps and Bruce Lee's kicks remind us of the persistent traces of the Japanese empire. Furthermore, I want to show that these failures of decolonization are exacerbated by the postwar Cold War system under American hegemony in the region. Not only is Gojira tamed into the "secure horror" (Tudor 1989) of Godzilla, Bruce Lee, in his last film, is also disciplined into a mainstream Hollywood kung-fu star. The politics associated with Gojira (antinuclear testing) and Bruce Lee (anti–Japanese imperialism) are erased, if not repressed, for sheer entertainment and ideological containment. In short, the monster and the dragon have been domesticated, Americanized, and depoliticized.

Why Does Gojira Always Return to Tokyo?

Gojira is a monster created by nuclear radiation exposure and inspired by the real event of *Daigo Fukuryū Maru*, a Japanese tuna-fishing boat exposed to the fallout of American hydrogen-bomb testing in the Bikini Atoll on March 1, 1954. More than simply a reflection of a historical event, the film is to be read and interpreted on several levels. As Japan's "first postwar media event," Barak Kushner (2006) has argued that *Gojira* was unprecedented in several ways in its historical emergence. It was the first film to signal the return of Japan to the international stage, the first postwar film freed from American Occupation censorship, and the first film to generate a franchise. Furthermore, for Kushner, *Gojira* represents "the perspective of a bridge between Japan's imperial war from 1931 to 1945 and the postwar" (41). Susan Napier, for instance, reads Gojira symptomatically as a "rewriting of history" that temporarily and emotionally inverts the power relations between Japan and the United States in popular culture (1993: 327). The film has the "good" Japanese scientist (Serizawa), the inventor of the Oxygen Destroyer, who sacrifices himself, not just for the nation (as during wartime) but for humanity, in order to defeat Gojira, the embodiment of "bad" American nuclear ambition. In this regard, Gojira represents what I call a "symbolic anti-Americanism" that not only enables Japan to claim moral superiority over the Americans, but its antinuclear and pacifist messages also align with a new emerging postwar Japanese identity that is democratic and peace-loving.[4]

Reading against the dominant interpretations of Gojira as antinuclear and antiwar, the Japanese literary critic Katō Norihiro (2010) argues that Gojira is the embodiment of the Japanese war dead who are unable to rest in peace, due to their ambiguous status as both victimizers and victims. Katō asks a simple question: "Why do King Kong and Gojira repeatedly return to NYC and Tokyo, respectively?" Using the Freudian notion of the uncanny, Katō reads both monsters as "something close to the heart, but repressed" (2010: 166). While they are ghastly and fearsome, once defeated or killed, along with precipitous relief and possible regret, Katō contends that there is also something that evokes sorrow. In the case of Gojira, the film serves as a "protective mechanism" of a Japanese unconscious that represses the duality of Gojira/war dead that continues to haunt the Japanese psyche as long as postwar Japanese society refuses to come to terms with its past, a symptom he has famously coined as *nejire*, or twistedness, in postwar Japan (1997). In the diegesis of the film, Katō likens the movements and the destruction of the Tokyo area by Gojira as reminiscent of the air raid during the war. Moving slowly, pausing at times, and twisting his body in pain, Gojira (and the Japanese war dead) seem to express literally, "Where is the nation that one has died for? Where did our motherland go?" (2010: 153).

Gojira repeatedly returns to Tokyo, in Katō's reading, precisely because postwar Japan has not squarely confronted its relationship with its war dead. These victims were mobilized believing in the value of sacrifice for the nation and the liberation of Asia. However, with Japan's defeat, a "conversion" took place in the national psyche from anti- to pro-Americanism. What was left unresolved by this conversion, according to Katō, was the relationship between those who survived the war, those who came to realize the new values of peace and democracy, and those who perished in the name of the holy war. The continued remaking of Gojira after fifty years and twenty-eight films is an attempt by the Japanese society to "sanitize, sterilize, neutralize and normalize" the uncanny represented by Gojira and Japan's war dead (2010: 169). In a rather whimsical conclusion to his analysis, Katō ponders whether, if he were to be asked to direct another Gojira film, he would have Gojira head over to the Yasukuni Shrine (the controversial site honoring Japan's war dead) and have Gojira "destroy Yasukuni!"

Katō's interpretation of Gojira follows the logic of his earlier and more controversial work, *Haisengoron* (On war defeat). In it, Katō argues that to offer an authentic, formal apology for the twenty million (non-Japanese) Asian victims of the Pacific War, it is first necessary for Japanese society to form a national subject via the process of mourning the three million Japanese war dead. Katō's logic is based on his reference to Japan's postwar "split personality," in which Dr. Jekyll apologizes for Mr. Hyde, who defends Japan's wartime aggression. This "twistedness" is the result of a postwar "conversion" where the Pacific war was refuted as a bad war, and the nation's relation to those who died in the name of liberating Asians was ignored (i.e., the Greater East Asian War). For bereaved families and others sympathetic to the war dead, the Yasukuni Shrine and its associated practices of worshipping the war dead became fertile ground for right-wing extremism. Hence, according to Katō, Japanese leftists and progressives are to be blamed for Yasukuni-type radicalism. Katō then invites progressives to honor Japan's own war deceased as a means to undercut the so-called Yasukuni logic. Only by collectively facing the uncanny and haunting figure of Gojira/war dead, and having Gojira destroy the Yasukuni Shrine, can Japan and its people get rid of their *nejire*. As Victor Koschmann and others have pointed out, Katō's rhetoric is inseparable from the conditions of Japan's two-decade-long recession. For Koschmann, "even the perceived need to apologize to other Asians for Japanese aggression and atrocities can be appropriated as the pretext for national mobilization" (2006: 123).

Katō's prescription amounts to an alibi for the Japanese government and ultimately results in a perpetual "deferral" of apologies and compensations from the Japanese government. Not only is there no guarantee that a "Japanese national subject" can cohere out of mourning the Japanese war dead, but also the formation of the national subject necessitates the construction and reification of "self" and "other" that would make any sincere reconciliation impossible. While I agree with Koschmann's critique of Katō's "prescription" to the problem, I do think that his analysis needs to be taken seriously. However, as I hope to elucidate throughout the rest of the book, the problem does not lie only in Japan's war responsibility. Instead, I want to suggest that it is the lack of "decolonization"—for both Japan and its former colonized—that has repressed or suppressed Japan's contradictory coloniality/modernity. Simply put, unlike some other colonial powers,

Japan's war defeat signaled the end of its empire. The ensuing Cold War and American hegemony that aided Japan's rapid economic recovery all contributed to the "forgetting" of colonial wounds. While the postcolonial (divided) nation-states of Taiwan and South Korea signed normalization treaties with Japan that supposedly resolved all reparations and compensations for Japan's military aggression, these states were driven by economic imperatives rather than by desires for a political reconciliation based on sincere and deep reflection. As a result of this incomplete or suspended decolonization and deimperialization, anti-Japanism remains a powerful sentiment in the region, though with intensities that vary from country to country whose state apparatuses often appropriate this sentiment to conceal or deflect domestic problems and social contradictions.

Why Does Bruce Lee Take Off His Shirt?

If Gojira represents the struggle to define Japan's postcoloniality and its "symbolic anti-Americanism" to rewrite history (that a Japanese scientist saves the day), Bruce Lee embodies the anticolonial, anti-Japanese sentiment that avenges centuries of Chinese (Asian) humiliations at the hands of imperialist powers. Just as Gojira elicits multiple readings, so does Bruce Lee. Yet as much as Lee represents, cinematically, anti-Japanism, this alone cannot explain his tremendous popularity in Japan even to this day. (A topic we shall return to later.) Steve Fore has rightly observed that, despite Lee's death in 1973, Lee remains the most potent icon of a cultural China and of a particular version of the Chinese nation and Chinese nationalism. What is important for the emergence of both Bruce Lee as an anti-imperialist heroic figure and Chinese nationalism is the historical coincidence between the rise of Lee in the cultural Chinese imaginary and the first Diaoyu controversy in the early 1970s. Fore relates the story of a 1996 incident around the disputed island that accentuates Lee's continued relevance in anti-Japanism. On September 26, 1996, a group of seventeen activists from Taiwan and Hong Kong, along with forty-two journalists, boarded a rusting freighter, *Kien Hwa no. Two*, to protest Japan's claim to the Diaoyu/Senkaku islands. This boarding was a result of a long-standing dispute that had come to a boiling point earlier that year (July 14) when the right-wing Japan Youth Association landed on one of the islets and built a five-meter-high, solar-powered, aluminum lighthouse, and requested that the Japanese Maritime Safety Agency designate it an official navigational signal. The protesters were monitored and intercepted by Japanese vessels. At around eight thirty in the morning of the 26th, five activists, including David Chan, a longtime Diaoyu activist, jumped into the water and attempted to swim from the boats to an islet as a symbolic gesture of reclaiming sovereignty. The unexpectedly rough water engulfed the activists; Chan drowned and was pronounced dead shortly afterward. One of the survivors was rescued by the Japanese coast guard and transported to a hospital in Okinawa. During his recuperation, he stated to the Hong Kong press that he wanted "to return to Hong Kong wearing either a traditional Chinese robe or a Bruce Lee T-shirt" (Fore 2001: 118).

Anti-Japanese movements in the early 1970s were largely organized and enacted in Sinophone areas outside of mainland China: Hong Kong, Taiwan, Southeast Asia, and among Chinese students in the United States.[5] Lee's films were banned in mainland China until the early 1980s, although rumor has it that Mao secretly admired his films. What this means is that current anti-Japanese sentiment in mainland China is a much later phenomenon than those of the 1970s (the topic of chapter 2), due to Cold War politics and uneven development between Chinese socialism and East Asian capitalism. Lee represents a *cultural* nationalism because it did not posit mainland China or its regime as representative of the amorphous and yet encompassing love for the imaginary homeland based on overcoming China's modern history of humiliation by foreign powers.

Of the four completed Bruce Lee films, *Fist of Fury* is arguably the most popular in East Asia. That the film has continued to be an inspiration even to this day in the Chinese cultural imaginary is evidenced by the plethora of remakes, parodies, sequels, and prequels by stars such as Jackie Chan, Stephen Chow, Jet Li, and Donnie Yen.[6] What is it about *Fist of Fury* that resonates with the Chinese-speaking audience and assures its longevity and afterlife, not unlike *Gojira*? I would like to suggest two possibilities. First, the film's historical setting, occupied Shanghai in the 1920s, marks the highpoint of China's century of humiliation. Western and Japanese imperialists not only defeated China and the Chinese materially, but also shamed the people, especially men, culturally. This is evidenced by two commonly held, although never verified, episodes represented by the derogatory phrases "The Sick Men of Asia" and "No Dogs or Chinese Allowed." Two memorable scenes encapsulate Lee's physical annihilation of these inscriptions, hence symbolically rejecting the sentiments of collective shame. Inside the Japanese *dōjō*, Lee not only returns "The Sick Men of

Asia" wooden frame to the Japanese, but also demolishes all the Japanese with martial art moves and the famous nunchaku sticks, accompanied by his distinct screech and stare. And as if to return the humiliation to the Japanese, he crumples the paper where "The Sick Men of Asia" was written and makes the Japanese eat it as they promised they would do when they brought the sign to the funeral of Lee's teacher. Once Lee proves to the Japanese imperialists that he, and by extension the Chinese people, is neither sick nor weak, but capable of vengeance and violence, Lee proceeds to confront the second representation of Chinese humiliation. Soon after he leaves the *dōjō*, Lee chances upon the "No Dogs or Chinese Allowed" sign hanging outside of the city park where Westerners are taking leisurely walks. As the Sikh guard points to the sign and the Japanese beckon him to enter the park as a dog, Lee leaps, and with his signature high kick shatters the sign, much to the astonishment of the Sikh guard and the Japanese colonialists. Lee is then cheered by Chinese bystanders. These powerful avenging scenes serve to allow the audience, especially the Chinese-speaking audience, to experience a catharsis heretofore repressed and unrealizable, and one that at least temporarily reverses the power relations between Japanese/Western imperialists and Chinese, not unlike the way Gojira allows Japanese viewers an opportunity to be on the winning side.

Another aspect of *Fist of Fury* that provides affective resonance with Chinese-speaking viewers is the reference to martyrdom. *Fist of Fury* ends with Lee's character, Chen Zhen, walking out of the martial art school in order to save the school from police and Japanese interrogation. In the memorable final scene, Lee struts out slowly to face the legion of police and soldiers with guns pointing at him, ready to fire. His character, chin held high, defiant and yet elegant, charges the crowd with his signature shriek, leaps up, and freezes in midair as we hear gunshots fired and the film ends. While it is presumed that Chen Zhen must have perished from the gunfire, the frozen frame points to a suspended state between life and death, a pause in history that retains the possibility of resistance. In short, Bruce Lee, or his martial representation of cultural Chineseness, not as a sick man of Asia or an equivalence to a canine, but as a reluctant and yet capable masculine presence, provided the necessary channel for overseas Chinese to project their long-held and repressed anguish and animosity toward Japanese and other imperialist powers. More importantly, *Fist of Fury is* also the film in which Lee, for the first time, takes off his shirt.

FIGURE I.I. Bruce Lee leaps in *Fist of Fury* (1974).

Some of the visual aesthetics of Lee are his smooth, quick kicks and punches; his usage of weapons (such as the nunchaku) not usually seen in traditional martial art films before he introduced them; and his signature screech. What sets him apart, however, from his predecessors (Jimmy Wang Yu) and successors (Jackie Chan, Jet Li, Donnie Yen) is his propensity to display his upper body, especially during fight scenes. Unlike the visual representation of other Asian male figures, Lee always deliberately takes off his shirt, displaying his chiseled physique. And the image of this body is not static. Instead, as Chris Berry has argued, Lee's body is a "transnational frame" that offers different interpretations in different times and in different places according to local circumstances. Furthermore, in a transnational framework, it becomes significant that the vehicle for the "triumph of the underdog" narrative is also a Chinese man and that the particular masculinity he embodies foregrounds the eroticized male body. Berry therefore argues that "Lee's body is an agonized one—caught in the double-bind of a compulsion to respond to modern American masculinity on one hand, and a homophobic and racially marked self-hatred that is a precondition for that ability to respond on the other." Berry also points to the history of Chinese masculinity—*wen* (the literary) and *wu* (the martial)—that defies the polarization of the Asian American understanding of masculinity (asexualized) and the Western expectation of feminization (2006: 219).

It is here where Lee's demonstrative showcasing of the body breaks away from all previous conventions in martial art films. Lee's hybridization of Chinese *wu* masculinity and American masculinity can be read as not separate from but closely tied to the various nationalist and anticolonial interpretations of the underdog narratives in his films (226). In short, the visibility of Lee's body is a startling contrast from the invisibility of male bodies of previous martial art stars. As Berry pointed out earlier, however, this masculinized body is also a Chinese body. The revelation of the body (when Lee is shirtless) follows a long-standing convention of Chinese prohibition, that of *ren* (to endure, to bear and forebear). The prohibition is the mechanism that builds up tensions and anticipations whereby the hero is instructed not to fight back. In the three Hong Kong–made films, the figures of the mother (*The Big Boss*), the school (*Fist of Fury*), and the uncle (*The Way of the Dragon*) all represent hierarchical relationships that prohibit Lee's characters to fight, or rather, to reveal his martial art expertise. The repression, of course, does not, and cannot, last long. Predictably, but with a considerable emotional outburst, Lee's characters display their superior skills and go on to defeat foes with the audience roaring approval and applauding. In short, this revelation of his expertise is frequently and characteristically accompanied by the removal of his shirt. This undressing undoes the Western perception of Chinese as the "sick men of Asia"—feeble, feminine, and feudal. Berry puts it succinctly: "The moment at which he can no longer turn the other cheek is not only marked by his engaging the enemy with the full force of his fury, in the typical *wu* manner. It is also when the shirt literally comes off and he bares his muscular upper body" (227).

It is important to underscore again that the martial body is also a Chinese body, or a racialized body: hence, the tremendous cathartic identification by the audience. Yet this identification, as Kwai-Cheung Lo has argued for people in Hong Kong when the films first appeared, is neither natural nor direct (1996: 104). Lee's popularity among Hong Kongers lies not so much in the people's desire for decolonization (as argued by M. T. Kato [2007], for instance), but in their desire for an imaginary China they can identify with. Put differently, it is not a specific Hong Kong identity that the audience craved, but a fantasized and void "China" or "Chineseness," that which suffered in the hands of the Westerners and the Japanese, that produces their identification with the "Chinese" hero represented by Lee. This fantasized China and symbolic anticolonialism, based on the nation's century of humiliation by foreign powers, are what make Lee's first three films speak to diasporic Chinese in Asia and beyond.

How Gojira Gets Trumped by Godzilla, and the Patriot Turns into a Secret Agent

Despite *Gojira*'s symbolic anti-Americanism and Lee's symbolic anti-colonialism, the representational struggles (and their political possibilities) were contained and tamed by the Cold War system and American hegemony. Two years after *Gojira*, in 1956, an Americanized version, better known as *Godzilla*, premiered in American theaters. Conforming to the established monster-flick genre that caters to the emerging youth audience in American suburbs, the production of *Godzilla* took tremendous liberty in editing, cutting, and transforming Gojira into Godzilla (Guthrie-Shimizu 2006). The free rein that American producers took with the Japanese *Gojira* is symptomatic of the power differential between the two nations in the Cold War era, as I discuss in more detail later. Whereas *Gojira* presented a not-so-veiled critique of hydrogen-bomb testing (hence of American violence), *Godzilla* suppressed the politics of nuclear weapons and American crimes against the Japanese population by excising thirty minutes of footage referencing Hiroshima and Nagasaki. And while the *Fifth Lucky Dragon* incident was still fresh in most people's consciousness when *Gojira* was shown in Japan, *Godzilla* was presented simply as an entertaining "secure horror."[7]

The asymmetrical power relations between the United States and Japan can be illustrated by the uncanny (or unconscious) gendered representations in the two films. Raymond Burr, as Steve Martin, an American reporter, was inserted into *Godzilla* to witness and describe the destruction caused by the menacing monster. An Asian security officer, Tomo Iwanaga (played by the Asian American actor Frank Iwanaga), is also slotted into the American remake as Burr's sidekick. It is the relationship between Martin and Iwanaga that deserves our attention here. In a parallel sequence in both films, we see the unintended but telling representation of the United States and Japan. In *Gojira*, the sequence begins with a villager ringing the bell to signal the appearance of the monster. As Dr. Yamane and his entourage of reporters and villagers climb the hill, they are confronted with the first appearance of Gojira. Startled and panicked,

FIGURE I.2. Ogata and Emiko embrace in *Gojira* (1954).

the group rush back down the hill. As they run for their lives, Emiko, Dr. Yamane's daughter, trips and falls. Almost immediately in the classic hero-saves-dame image, Ogata, her love interest, comes to her rescue, holding her up in a lovers' embrace as they both look worriedly in the direction of the monster.

In *Godzilla*, the same sequence is repeated, but with a twist. Before Emiko falling, we see Burr's Asian male sidekick, Iwanaga, falls down as well. And just as Ogata comes to Emiko's aid, we see Burr's burly character lift the helpless and hapless Iwanaga off the ground. The uncanny parallelism represented here is not a homosexual embrace, but a distinctly heteronormative enactment of gender and sexual differences. The large Burr character towering over the small meek Asian male in the black and white film resembles the iconic photograph of General MacArthur standing majestically next to the short and stiff Emperor Hirohito immediately after Japan's surrender.

In that photograph, as in *Godzilla*, Japan is feminized, emasculated, and made to be a supportive partner of America's new hegemony in anti-Communist East Asia. This "marriage" and its subsequent reverse course allowed Japan to recuperate and recover as an economic power under the

FIGURE I.3. Burr helps an Asian man in *Godzilla* (1956).

guidance and protection of American militarism that, along with the co-operation of similarly American-led authoritarian regimes in South Korea and Taiwan, virtually relieved Hirohito's and Japan's wartime and colonial responsibilities as well as America's own atrocities and war crimes, hence nullifying decolonization. The American empire simply replaced the Japanese empire. The critical valences in *Gojira* were short-lived. After the surprising success of the film, and in conjunction with the rising consumerism and depoliticized culture, Gojira became a franchise. The first *Gojira*, much like its American counterpart, succumbs to the logic of capitalism and American militarism, vanquished in the deep sea and never to be awakened again.

It is well known that Lee left for Hong Kong to pursue his film career due to racism in America. Furthermore, his success in Asia had much to do with his films' appeal to the "underdog" persona and to the anti-imperialist (Japanese and whites) and anti-villain (overseas Chinese bosses) sympathies in the first three films he made in Hong Kong. It is, therefore, ironic that *Enter the Dragon*, Lee's breakout film in terms of worldwide distribution and visibility, was a Hollywood production. *Enter the Dragon*, as many have observed, while set in Hong Kong and featuring some of

FIGURE I.4. Hirohito and General MacArthur meeting for the first time on September 27, 1945. Photo by Lt. Gaetano Faillace.

his more famous philosophizing on martial art, is less about his previous cultural and national personas than it is simply a well-crafted and entertaining story of a martial art tournament and a spy narrative. Instead of being a country bumpkin, an underclass figure, or a patriot, Lee plays the role of a James Bond–like secret agent who infiltrates the tournament in order to bust a drug ring, free the slaves, and defeat the Chinese boss on the desolate island where the tournament is held. Although not as dramatic as the *Gojira/Godzilla* sequence I mentioned earlier, the transformation of Lee from an underdog patriot to a martial art teacher and secret agent is obviously a nod to Hollywood's perception of how to use Lee's kung-fu skills with a familiar Cold War narrative represented by the James Bond franchise.

In the famous *sifu/sensei*/teacher–student/disciple sequence that later martial art films, notably *The Karate Kid* franchise, followed and emulated, Lee is seen instructing a young practitioner. A few exchanges between them ensue, and we witness the other side of Lee, the *wen*, or literary, aspect of the kung-fu master described by Berry earlier, a character that is devoid in three of Lee's Hong Kong films. With his typical Sino-English accent, Lee retorts the student: "Don't think, feeeeeel," and "It's like a finger pointing away to the moon. Don't concentrate on the finger or you will miss all that heavenly glory," as the young disciple learns not just martial arts but a life lesson. In the global circuit of Lee's first Americanized production, the underclass, undereducated, and anti-imperialist characters that galvanized the audience in Asia gave way to a cosmopolitan, philosophizing secret agent doing clandestine work for the U.S. government.

It is important to underscore here the parallelism between the United States and Japan in their timing of the reception of Lee. Unlike the uncanny gendered relations in *Gojira/Godzilla* that mirrored the asymmetrical power relations between America and Japan in the immediate postwar era, the similarity in these nations' respective interests in Lee points to the complicity between the United States and Japan and their differential power relations vis-à-vis Asia. The belated entry of Lee's films into Western and Japanese markets underscores the disconnect between Japan and its Asian neighbors in the postwar Cold War period. Lee's first three films in the early 1970s were extremely successful in Hong Kong, Taiwan, and Southeast Asia. While Lee's popularity became global in scale later, from Harlem to Torino, from London to Beirut (Prashad 2001), its temporality was not shared evenly worldwide. As Yomota Inuhiko (2005) has observed, compared to the rest of the (third) world, Lee's films were relatively late screening in Japan. The first showing of *Enter the Dragon* was in December 1973, five months after Lee's untimely death. Unlike in most Asian countries, the first Lee film to enter Japan was the American-produced one (Warner Brothers) and was in English.[8] His films were advertised as "oriental action films from the U.S., and words like 'kung fu' and 'Bruce Lee' were written in *katakana*, the Japanese scripts for foreign words" (2005: 20). In contrast, South Korea reads Lee in *hangul* pronunciation, Yi So Ryon. What this historical "accident" signifies is that unlike "Asia" or other "third worlds," the Japanese reception of Lee was much more closely aligned with the United States, further underscoring the temporal and spatial asymmetry between Japan and "Asia."[9] In short, in the late 1960s and early 1970s, Japan simply did not have a shared consciousness with the rest of "Asia." To borrow Johannes Fabian's (2002) much-used word, Japan lacked "co-evalness" with Asia. The reversed order and American-ized reception of Lee's films in Japan mitigated Japanese viewers' reaction to the anti-Japanese and cultural nationalist sentiments in films like *Fist of Fury*. Japanese viewers dismissed the portrayals of Japanese villains in the film as caricatures and misrepresented stereotypes, pointing out the awkwardly placed wigs and the actors wearing the Japanese *hakama* backward. In short, anti-Japanese elements in Lee's film were laughed away and its historical significance displaced and repressed. The Japanese reception of *Fist of Fury* contrasts dramatically with the film's long-standing impact on anti-Japanese sentiments and nationalist feeling. While Lee kicked and punched his way into the hearts of the Japanese audience, his naked torso no longer bears the scars of anti-Japanism or anti-imperialism.

As cultural representations, Gojira and Bruce Lee are symptomatic of the possibilities of resistance within the political impossibility of the post-war Cold War system in East Asia. As symbolic anti-Americanism and anti-Japanism, respectively, in contexts where actual oppositions are not available or allowed, they represent sites of desire and fantasy, and they are projections of social anxieties that cannot be "fixed" in historical reality. That the problem of unresolved decolonization—Gojira as the Japanese war dead and Bruce Lee as Chinese cultural nationalism—is still with us today only points to the political quagmire that continues to obstruct any process of reconciliation or integration in the region. The colonial and decolonial questions are not simply about the past. As Arif Dirlik has cautioned, the "preoccupation with colonialism and its legacies makes for an exaggerated view of the hold of the past over contemporary realities and an obliviousness to the reconfiguration of past legacies by contemporary restructuration of power—especially changes in the practices of capitalism and the nation-state that have already called forth a reconsideration of the colonial past" (2002: 429). Issues of colonialism and imperialism in the East Asian context, in the form of anti-Japanism, I argue in the chapters that follow, are intrinsically connected to the increased apprehension over economic disparity in postsocialist China, demands for justice against patriarchal nationalism in South Korea, and the reassertion of cultural identities in post–martial law Taiwan. However, in the case of Taiwan, anti-Japanism also implies its repressed Other, pro-Japanism. These sentiments are neither culturalist nor timeless. They are conditioned by changing historical conjunctures and mediated through cultural representations. It is my contention that these contrary feelings toward "Japan" have less to do with the actual Japan or the Japanese empire, and more to do with projections and mobilizations around local crises and anxieties. Put simply, anti-Japanism (or pro-Japanism, in the case of Taiwan) remains palpable in the collective psyche of East Asia because it resonates with the failed decolonization of the Japanese empire *and* it galvanizes nationalist sentiments for coping with the growing precarity under global capitalism today.

It is not surprising that "nationalism" provides the content for the cinematic form to which Gojira (anti-Americanism) and Bruce Lee (anti-Japanism) are rendered legible, given that there are no other forms of resistance available. I have placed "nationalism" in quotation marks to denote the complication of the theorization of nationalism, more appropriately nationalist sentiment, surrounding Gojira and Bruce Lee. The goal of the chapters that follow is to point to the limits of nationalism in relation to anti-Japanism and gesture toward a subnational and transnational articulation of decolonization.

TWO. "Japanese Devils": The Conditions
and Limits of Anti-Japanism in China

With their pervasive visuality and virtuality, the demonstrations against Japan in several Chinese cities in 2005 inaugurated a new era of anti-Japanism. These mass rallies were widely televised through the airwaves and were YouTubed and videocasted on the internet; the protests were mobilized by cellphones and debated in chat rooms and online fora. Bloggers and vloggers continued to post opinions, movie clips, sound files, and flash videos about the anti-Japan movements well after the crackdown on the demonstrations by the Chinese authorities. The predominance of the visual and virtual flooded the public with scenes and images of Chinese fervor and unmitigated anger toward Japan. A Japanese news video showed a tearful Chinese woman in Shanghai driving in a Japanese car as she is pelted with eggs and profanity by a mob of mostly young male protesters. She begs for the crowd to let her leave while the camera pans to the small "Boycott Japanese Products" sticker on her rear window. Another one of the several thousands of random images posted on the internet shows a little boy sitting on his father's shoulders holding a toy machine gun with banners of "Down with Japanese Militarism" waving in the background. Still another photograph shows a boy holding a poster with the writing "Do Not Forget National Shame!" A flash video that mixes rap music, an animated cartoon, and grisly photos of the Nanjing Massacre urges every Chinese to avenge national humiliation by killing all Japanese.

The 2005 demonstrations fizzled as quickly as they erupted, largely due to the Chinese state's concern that the protests not run amok and cause irreparable damage to its bilateral relationship with Japan. Yet the events of 2005 offer a number of new paradigms for thinking about political protests in general and anti-Japanism in China in particular. First, in the age of the internet and new media, political movements are necessarily multiscalar—local, national, regional, and global—and their organizations less hierarchical and centralized, yet more rhizomatic and dispersed. Multimedia and mobile technologies such as computers, cellphones, and video cameras cannot only document in the traditional sense of the word, but also Photoshop, transmit, and re-signify the events in unpredictable and unintended ways. Blogs, chat rooms, and video gaming become the new sites of political warfare where fighting words, hurtful images, and simulated killings are interactively produced, circulated, and consumed, and where "intent," "truth," and "facts" are bracketed and deferred.

Second, unlike the mostly student-led protests against Japan over the textbook controversy in the 1980s, which were confined to university campuses, the 2005 events were mobilized and participated in by China's emerging middle-class professionals. The protests took place in major urban centers amid high-rises, shopping malls, and open boulevards. These new images of China's "peaceful rise" appeared radically incongruent with most Japanese peoples' stereotypical impressions of China as an underdeveloped Communist nation. But the 2005 events presented China in ways that shattered conventional Japanese ideas of China that had been consolidated in the postwar era. As Mizoguchi Yūzō (2005) has argued, this disjuncture between the actually existing China and Japan's perception of it points to the historical fact that Japan does not have a shared experience with the global south and, additionally, points to the reality that Japan's conceptualization of Asia is utterly out of date.[1]

Third, the outpouring of emotion by the protesters on cityscapes and cyberspaces—anger, outrage, zealousness, and even pleasure—requires us to take emotion, passion, hope, or sheer delight seriously and to recognize the power of some of the more alarming forms of popular nationalist sentimentality. To recognize these affective dimensions, as well as the interpretative dimensions, of political mobilization is to acknowledge a shift from memory and trauma to passion and indignation, thus acknowledging the way that historical events are re-membered in people's popular consciousness. In short, the geopolitical must be analyzed, understood, and theorized along with the biopolitical.

Critical colonial studies has alerted us to the numerous cultural technologies—images, metaphors, narratives, classifications, etc., or what David Spurr (1993) calls "the rhetoric of empire"—employed by a colonial discourse that has framed and perpetuated a false conception of the inferiority of colonized and imperialized subjects. But what has received less scholarly attention are the ways in which the colonized perform "excitable speeches" (Butler 1997) against the oppressor, or utilize incendiary images to represent the colonizer's barbarity, or remind us of the oppressor's record of violence and atrocities.

In this chapter I would like to look at one instance in Sino-Japanese relations: the epithet *"riben guizi"* (Japanese devils) in Chinese popular culture. I argue that this "hate word" performs an affective politics of recognition stemming from an ineluctable trauma of imperialist violence. Most important, I argue that anti-Japanism in China is less about Japan than about China's own self-image mediated through its asymmetrical power relations with Japan throughout its modern history. Finally, by analyzing Matsui Minoru's documentary *Riben Guizi* (Japanese devils; 2001), I suggest that, by assuming the racial epithet, the Japanese director and the veterans interviewed in the film perform an important self-critical and courageous testimony to Japanese war crimes. The perpetrators' confessions and admissions open up a much-needed space of dialogical possibility between victimizers and victims.

Guizi in the Chinese Imperium

Together with *"xiao riben"* (little Japan), *"riben guizi"* is perhaps one of the most casually and frequently utilized phrases in Chinese popular discourse, referring condescendingly to the Japanese. It is an enunciation that is politically and socially useful precisely to the extent that it is excitable and conjures emotions of disdain, deprecation, hatred, and envy. However, unlike hate speech where the recognition is an imposing of a name or language upon another that perpetuates subordination, these anti-Japan epithets attempt to overturn the subordinated position of the Chinese vis-à-vis the Japanese, at least symbolically. In this sense, *"xiao riben"* and *"riben guizi"* refer less to Japan and the Japanese and instead invoke a ritualized context that confirms (or reaffirms) a concept of Chinese superiority over an inferior and barbaric Japan or Japanese. Much like the contemporary global consumption of Japanese mass culture—where the consumption is not about Japan as an identity, but about *the idea* of Japan conjured in the minds of the consumers—anti-Japanism tells us more about the subject positions of anti-Japan enunciators than about Japan itself (Ko 2003). In this sense, these denigrating references can only constitute an internal conversation; its passion and affect are produced, circulated, and consumed ritualistically within an enclosed community. (Such internal referencing often comes undone with a sense of embarrassment when Chinese speakers suddenly realize that the Japanese addressee actually understands Chinese.)

"*Guizi*" derives from the word "*gui*," meaning ghost or spirits of the deceased, a word that also evokes notions of monstrosity or the unknown. "*Guifang*" or "*guiguo*" has come to signify distant and foreign territories where "barbarians" resided. In the era of high imperialism, the modern form "*guizi*" was used widely as a derogatory term for foreigners, especially after the Opium Wars. During the Qing dynasty, it primarily referred to Westerners from across the ocean, as the phrase "*yang guizi*" (foreign devils) would designate. It is important to recognize here that the "Chinese"/ "*guizi*" differentiation relies on a premodern cartography of the civility-barbarity (*hua-yi*) binary that differs from the modern Western colonial hierarchy of racial classification. Imperial Sinocentrism relied more on a civilizational discourse for its hegemony, whereas imperialist Eurocentrism relied on a discourse of race to legitimize its civilizing mission. With the Japanese invasion of China proper, the Japanese came to be known as *dongyang guizi* (eastern devils) and *riben guizi* as differentiated from *yang guizi*. It was only during the War of Resistance against Japan and after its victory that *guizi* became synonymous with "Japanese" and has remained a popular derision to this day.

The Japanese, however, were not always considered devilish even while they engaged in aggression against China. As Takeda Masaya (2005) has shown, from the first Sino-Japanese war until the War of Resistance, the preferred term to describe the Japanese was "*wo*" as in "*woren*" (people of servitude, people of small stature) and "*woguo*" (land of the people of servitude, land of the people of small stature), terms that have been documented in classical Chinese texts since the first century. Again, it is important to underscore here that the Self/Other distinction is not based on the modern notion of sovereign nation-states or peoples, but determined by the *hua-yi* cosmology of Sinocentrism. According to Takeda, from around the tenth century, the official discourse on Japan has shifted away from using "*wo*," which has been replaced by the more geographically oriented nomenclature of "*riben*," "*ribenguo*," and "*dongying*." Only with the inception of the Sino-Japanese war did "*wo*" make an auspicious return to once again designate China's eastern enemy. Although Takeda does not discuss the reason for this revival of "*wo*," one can argue that it constituted a haughty attempt to sustain the Sinocentric model of the regional order. The propagandistic superiority of the Qing army and the cultural inferiority of the Japanese, depicted in the Dianshizhai Pictorial that Takeda relied on for his study, attest to the desire to maintain a semblance of order in the Chinese imperium that had been decomposing since the Opium Wars and had completely collapsed after the Sino-Japanese war. By the time of the War of Resistance, "*wo*" almost completely disappears from the popular lexicon and is replaced by "*guizi*" and other modern epithets such as "invaders," "enemy," "Japanese bandits," and so on. What I would like to suggest is that the specific denomination of "*woren*" and "*woguo*" to designate the Japanese people and Japan during the Sino-Japanese war served as a transitional phase from the Chinese empire based on the *hua-yi* system to the colonial empire based on modern nation-states.

The *hua-yi* order is a political geography that differentiates the *hua* (the Han Chinese people, or civility) from that of *yi* (the eastern tribes of ancient China, or barbarity). The *hua-yi* order is not static. As the territory of China expanded throughout its history, it is conceivable and perceivable that the *yi* can be "assimilated" into the *hua*. The *hua*, representing the center of the universe, however, cannot be challenged or usurped (Sun Ge 2010: 18).[2] In short, the *hua* is irreplaceable, and the references to the Japanese as *woren* and *woguo* continue this Sinocentric thought of managing differences in the Chinese empire.

However, in Japan, Confucian scholars conceived of a more fluid notion of the *hua-yi* order. Instead of a geographically relativized center-peripheral order between civility and barbarity, the terms "*hua*" and "*yi*" are understood as two "measures of political culture" that are interchangeable. Ogyū Sorai, for instance, has argued that *hua* and *yi* are not fixed categories, but have potentials for *hua* to degenerate to *yi* or for *yi* to elevate to *hua*, depending on whether or not each adheres to the ancient teachings of the sage kings (quoted in Sun Ge 2010: 18). The emergence of the term "*guizi*" during the War of Resistance came to signify not only the specific modern notion of Japan and the Japanese but also the imagined community of China. In short, if "*wo*" still signified a Sinocentric understanding of Japan's (subordinate) place in the Chinese cosmology, then *"guizi"* points to the end of that worldview and China's tacit realization of its (subordinate) positionality within the newly reconfigured modern imperialist system. In short, by designating and delimiting a "premodern" Sinocentric worldview, *"wo"* has become anachronistic.

Guizi in the War of Resistance

In his 1937 speech, "The Meaning of the War of Resistance," Chen Duxiu argues that the War of Resistance is not a temporary emotional reaction, but has a long historical meaning. He places the anti-Japanese war in a series of revolutionary attempts at political changes in modern Chinese history: from Li Hongzhang's Self-Strengthening Movement to Kang Youwei and Liang Qichao's Wuxu Reform, from Sun Yat-sen's Republican revolution to the Northern Expedition. Furthermore, Chen defines the historical significance of the war within the context of global imperialism, and he purposefully differentiates Japanese imperialists from the Japanese people in the anti-imperialist war. He writes:

> This anti-Japanese war is not based on temporary emotion or national vengeance, and [is] definitely not fought for empty phrases such as justice, humanitarianism or peace. Instead, it is a revolutionary war of the oppressed nation/people against imperialism. The target of our resistance is Japanese imperialism. However, it is the Japanese imperialists and not the Japanese people [that we fight] because those who oppress us are not the Japanese people, but [the] Japanese military and its government. The historical meaning of the war is to release us from the oppression and constraints of imperialism in order to complete China's independence and unification. (5)

For Chen, the war is not to be apprehended as one between governments in Nanking and Tokyo, but as an anti-Japanese imperialist war that requires the mobilization of the entire Chinese people. Victory against Japanese imperialism will also deter other imperialist nations from further oppressing the Chinese people. From Chen's socialist/internationalist perspective, it is crucial to distinguish imperialists from ordinary people who also suffer from the ills of imperialism. This distinction is, of course, later famously reiterated by Premier Zhou Enlai in the 1972 Communiqué between the two governments as part of their normalizing of diplomatic relations.

The distinction between Japanese imperialists and the Japanese populace can also be seen in the so-called anti-Japanese comics published during the War of Resistance. Along with the numerous caricatures of bucktoothed and mustached Japanese militarists, there are also comics depicting the suffering of the Japanese people during the long drawn-out war: the intense rationing of foodstuffs, the return of fallen soldiers' ashes, and the overall sacrifice of the common people. In many of these comics, what is accentuated is the evil and exploitative nature of Japanese militarism alongside the suffering of the increasingly defeated Japanese people. As a visual medium created in conjunction with the war effort, anti-Japanese comics underscored the eventual doom of the Japanese military operation as a result of the prolonged resistance of the Chinese people. The portrayal of the Chinese is understandably heroic and resilient, with the only exception being that of the collaborators, who are often depicted as greedy and doglike in their subservience.

If the enemy has been clearly defined as Japanese imperialists and not the Japanese people, its most immediate manifestation becomes the Japanese soldiers. It is within this context of identifiable enemy combatants that popular songs during the War of Resistance spell out who their enemies are (Sun Shen 1995). The audio medium of popular songs, like the comics mentioned above, plays an important affective and political role in the period of mobilization. Marching melodies accompanied by patriotic lyrics celebrate the history and the struggles of the Chinese people. Most of the songs of the period praise the spirit of the Chinese people in resisting Japanese imperialism, urge the people to rise up and continue to resist their enemies, glorify the Chinese people and the nation, proclaim the dawn of a new China, and so on. There are also songs that refer specifically to the Japanese. In these songs, Japan and the Japanese are called, variously, "enemies" (*diren*), "devils" (*guizi*), "Japanese devil" (*riben gui*), "bandits" (*rikou*), "Japanese imperialism" (*riben diguo zhuyi*), "little Japan" (*xiao dongyang, xiao riben*), "Japanese military" (*rijun*), and "invaders" (*qinluezhe*). Of all the incendiary references to the Japanese, "*guizi*" and "*riben gui*" elicit the most emotion in songs that are associated directly with killing the Japanese. In lines such as "a large sword aimed at the heads of the *guizi*," "expel the *guizi* from our territory," "kill the *guizi* and chop off their heads," and "fight the *guizi* to the end," "*guizi*," more than simply "enemy" or "Japanese army," stirs anger and passion for the acts (real or imagined) of killing the devils. Whereas "Japanese imperialism" or "Japanese military" are recited in songs lauding the tenacity and bravery of the Chinese army, "Japanese devils" incites specific acts of violence against the Japanese soldiers. What we can conclude from looking at these comics and popular songs is that with the ensuing war on the Chinese mainland, the imperial term *"wo"* gives way to the more specific designation of Japanese military and imperialists. *"Guizi"* emerges in this context of global imperialism along with other epithets describing Japanese militarism with the added emotion and sentimentality linked to necropolitics. However, care is taken to differentiate the Japanese people from Japanese imperialists, a sentiment that continues into the socialist era.

Guizi in the Socialist Imaginary

In the postwar socialist era, memories of the War of Resistance remain vivid and important in the legitimization of the Chinese Communist state. The War of Resistance against the Japanese was critical for both the global struggle of anti-imperialism and the unification of China. The war is an achievement claimed by both the Communists and the nationalists as the culmination of the Chinese people's resilience and the symbol of Chinese nationalism. For the Communist Party, after years of struggle against both the Japanese and the nationalists, the War of Resistance was crucial in establishing its own legitimacy. A number of popular films based on the themes of anti-Japanese struggle were produced and widely viewed in the 1950s and 1960s. These so-called anti-Japan films ostensibly re-created the Communists' struggle against the Japanese, valorizing their guerrilla tactics and socialist ideology. In other words, these anti-Japan films are less about Japan than about the Chinese state in its contemporary formation. Furthermore, although *"guizi"* and *"riben guizi"* are used casually to refer to the Japanese in these films, the terms tend to portray the Japanese devils as stereotypical, farcical figures. They are not figures to be feared, but ridiculed. Their demises are often exaggerated and even comical, soliciting laughter from the audience rather than indignation, as we have seen during the actual War of Resistance. The comic and at times absurd representations allow people to laugh away the trauma of war (Xu 2007: 66).

Set during the height of the resistance against the Japanese, classic films like *Landmine Warfare* (1962) and *Tunnel Warfare* (1965) extol socialist virtues of collectivism, populism, gender equality, self-reliance, and guerrilla strategies. As the titles of the films suggest, common people, usually villagers and peasants, ingenuously utilize indigenous technologies and landscapes—using a woman's long hair to trigger a mine or digging and connecting individual underground tunnels to hide and sabotage the Japanese army. People's struggles are complemented and reinforced by the Eighth-Route Army to further consolidate the cooperation and collaboration between common people and the Communists. It is this synergy that allows the Chinese resistance to eventually defeat the better-equipped modern military of Japanese imperialism.

Another recurring motif in these films is the presence of Chinese collaborators. The role of the traitor (*hanjian* or *zougou*) is crucial in delineating or differentiating the "good" from the "bad" Chinese. Collaborators continue to serve as the negative example of otherwise heroic Chinese subjectivities. The traitor characters are also utilized to express thoughts of the Japanese and relay their orders as interpreters and subservient go-betweens.

The *guizi* represented in these films are typically and singularly a captain or a commander of an army troop that is trying to attack a village and subjugate the villagers. These Japanese characters derive from the evil-looking, authoritarian, and cunning representations that first emerged in comics during the War of Resistance. They often grunt in unintelligible Japanese and personify the brutality of Japanese imperialism en masse. As expected, these commanders will face their demise at the end of the film while the audience celebrates the heroic victory of the Chinese people. What is of interest here is the often humorous, if not absurd, manner in which the Japanese villains die. The films end with marching songs that celebrate victory and refer to the Japanese as generic "invaders" (*qinluezhe*), although "*guizi*" is the common usage in the dialogue.

In both *Landmine Warfare* and *Tunnel Warfare*, the Japanese imperialists are not killed by individual soldiers, but through imaginary collective efforts. In the final scene of *Landmine Warfare*, Captain Nakano escapes as his horse is shot by a woman warrior. He stumbles onto a large boulder inscribed with the words "Suppress Demon Rock," lying by the side of the only road into the village. He sees a tall wooden tablet with "grave of the invaders" written on it and sees phantoms of bombs surrounding him like ghosts. He explodes as he tries to fend off the bombs by swinging wildly with his sword. The camera then cuts to the battlefield accompanied by a victorious song celebrating the people's ingenuity and resilience against the invaders.

A similar demise awaits the Japanese captain in *Tunnel Warfare*. After being trapped in a large cave by the guerrilla fighters, he is asked several times to drop his weapon, a typical bushido sword. The captain refuses and we hear a round of bullets being fired. The scene then cuts to an open field where the protagonist grabs him and has him witness the victorious celebration of the Chinese people. A celebratory scene ensues with beating music lauding the courage of the people against the invaders. What is important here is that the demise of a *singular* representation of Japanese evil is engendered through the *collective* valor and inventiveness of the Chinese people. Contrary to the downfall of the collaborators, who are usually eliminated by an identifiable Chinese character, the Japanese devil has to be symbolically exterminated through a united, communal effort.

What is constructed by the caricature of "the Japanese devils" is the heroic and positive memory of the War of Resistance. The comical, absurd portrayal of Japanese military leaders only serves to accentuate the triumphant and forward-looking characterization of a collective Communist endeavor. In the period of socialist nation-building, these *guizi* are only props to uphold the resilience and ingenuity of the Chinese people under the leadership of Mao and the Communist Party. For the Chinese, the history of the Second World War *is* the history of the War of Resistance against Japan, and that is vital to the Chinese self-image after decades of "national humiliation." For them the war represented a turning point between old and new China and ushered in the victory of socialism. It was a patriotic struggle of the whole of the Chinese people and revealed the importance of unity among all Chinese. It was also of world-historical significance because it was part of a worldwide struggle against fascism (Dirlik 1991: 51).

Guizi in Postsocialist Nationalism

This positive history of the War of Resistance in the 1950s and 1960s gradually gave way to the negative history of China's victimization in the 1980s and 1990s (Callahan 2007: 2010). The anti-Japan war became the signature of China's unity and the Communists' legitimacy in the postwar Cold War era. However, the rapid decomposition of the socialist economy since the 1970s required a different ideology to cope with the inequality and discontent caused by China's embrace of a market economy in the era of postsocialist globalization. There were already signs in the mid-1980s that the post-Mao reforms had run into trouble, and nationalist sentiment provided one means of reinvigorating the struggle for development. Along with Japan's own sense of asymmetry between its economic and political power—manifested in the textbook and Yasukuni controversies—popular nationalism emerged, now bearing more effects of China's suffering, culminating in the Nanjing Massacre.[3] The shift from socialism to nationalism became part of a delicate balancing act between the state's tacit approval of various anti-Japanese demonstrations and people's rousing emotions. Anti-Japanism in the 1980s and 1990s therefore served both to contain an emerging Japanese nationalism and to legitimize state power in the wake of massive economic reforms and popular discontent.

In the 1980s, anti-Japan demonstrations usually took the form of student protests and were largely confined to university campuses. In 2005 the protests broke out on a national scale and were mobilized and sustained by the internet and new media technologies. The internet and mobile devices, such as cellphones, have increasingly become an important arena for political activity, and this is a general phenomenon of the so-called network society. However, this technology is also becoming an integral part of commerce, communication, entertainment, and activism in the so-called developmental states. Its anarchic quality, nonlinear structure, and relatively open and transnational properties allow any users with access, at least theoretically, to voice their political opinions regarding local issues or global affairs. Technology, however, is social and despite its seemingly neutral and universal mechanism, its uses and effects are overdetermined by the specific cultural and historical contexts of its users. The internet culture has prompted various interpretations regarding the rise of popular nationalism in both Japan and China, especially in relation to the younger generation who are usually chided for their lack of historical consciousness. Rumi Sakamoto and Matt Allen (2007), for instance, have argued persuasively that one should be careful not to equate the growing popularity of anti-Asian manga in Japan with the rise of nationalism among young people there. The popularity of titles such as the inflammatory *Kenkanryū* (Hating the Korean wave) is driven not by young nationalist zealots who support the author's denigration of Korea and the Koreans, but by netizens who were disgusted by the seemingly colluded censorship of the manga, which was first published as a web comic by major publishers. The netizens mobilized a mass campaign so that *Kenkanryū* appeared at the top of Amazon's top ten list before the manga was even published, generating tremendous buzz for the work that traditional advertisers can only dream of.

The situation is, however, quite different in China. Internet expansion, as Jack Qiu (2004) has argued, is part of an explicit effort to rebuild the nation via the acquisition of technological competence in China as a developmental state (106). This techno-nationalism has a long tradition and was a key goal of Chinese leaders from Sun Yat-sen to Mao. While the Chinese state tried to employ computer networks primarily in the economic domain, grassroots user networks continue to transform the new technology from an abstract cyberspace to a meaningful place of social significance. Multitudes of grassroots formations—web-based nationalist movements, hacker alliances, youth cultures, gay and lesbian groups, and dissident uses of the internet via diverse channels such as chat rooms, online gaming, and peer-to-peer technologies—have given rise to a kaleidoscope of the intricate interplay among myriad social forces in the network of Chinese netizens (102).

Online protests in China first emerged in 1996, coordinated by Peking University's untitled Bulletin Board System station, focusing on the Japanese occupation of the Diaoyu islands in September. Since then, major online movements have targeted Indonesia (summer 1998), NATO (May 1999), Taiwan (July 1999), Japan (January 2000 and February to March 2001), and the United States (April to May 2001) (Qiu 2004: 116). These online activities typically arise within the first week of a crisis to coordinate mobilization and devise aggressive efforts. Interestingly, more rapid than the formation of online patriotic alliances was the speedy evaporation of many movements because of pressure from wary state authorities. This sudden emergence and rapid demise suggest that grassroots nationalism in China's cyberspace remains a short-term political spasm rather than an organized mode of citizen participation or a sustainable social force. Nonetheless, according to Qiu, "A nationalist discourse permeates Chinese political arenas on the Internet and remains central to the shaping of cultural identity at the *personal* level because, unlike modernist ideologies on the left or the right, it is the only state-promoted narrative framework that appeals to the majority of netizens" (116).

Other than debates on chat rooms and in blogs, the internet makes possible a combination of text, image, and sound, and it creates sites that provide more than text-based representations. Videocasts, podcasts, and flash movies are constantly being produced, mixed, cut and pasted, and consumed, blurring the boundaries between political activism and entertainment. What has emerged during and after the 2005 anti-Japanese protest is the proliferation of flash-based shorts on the internet that variously aimed at humiliating the Japanese and promoting nationalist sentiments. Among these brief movies, "*riben guizi*" or "*guizi*" has become a common denomination for referring to the Japanese that represents a crucial difference from earlier formulations. As we have seen, a deliberate attempt was made to differentiate the Japanese imperialist from the Japanese people throughout most of China's modern history. What postsocialist popular nationalism promotes, incites, and conflates are the heretofore distinct categories of Japan and the Japanese. It is no longer the imperialists per se, but the Japanese people who are national enemies. Whereas in the earlier periods, "*guizi*" was intended to accentuate the positivity of the War of Resistance and the socialist revolution, now "*guizi*" is directed against explicit enemy figures, that of Japan and the Japanese people.

Let me cite two examples. The internet game "Da Guizi" (Whac-a-Devil) follows the format of the popular Whac-a-Mole game popular in video arcades.[4] At the start prompt, the user is presented with a grid made of four by four rows of what look like tunnels with animated Japanese soldiers popping in and out like moles. The user is instructed to whack the soldiers by moving and right-clicking the mouse. Before continuing with the game, the main page shows on the left a Japanese soldier swaying back and forth from a rope tied to a red star above that represents China. On the right are texts that explain the rationale of the game. They speak of attaining national victory and independence through the War of Resistance after immense human and material loss—thirty-five million dead and injured. Yet the hard-fought victory is confronting a new reality today—Japan's encroaching military buildup, the shameless claims to the Diaoyu islands, the refusal to admit to the Nanjing Massacre, and so forth. The game then proclaims that "every shameless act made us finally recognize the [perception of] 'Chinese psychology' [支那精神] held by every Japanese and the soul of Japanese militarism." Unlike the earlier concerted effort to separate Japanese militarism from the Japanese people, today's anti-Japanism collapses the two into one common foe.

The flash movie "Resist Japan and Whack the Devils" (抗日打鬼子), with the English heading "Kill Them Together," provides another instance of equating "*guizi*" with the Japanese people in cyberspace.[5] Combining animation and rap, the short movie implores the Chinese to take revenge on the shameless Japanese and express their patriotism. In a four-minute clip, it reflects on the long history of Japan's subservient position in the China-centered world, Japan's invasion of China, the Nanjing Massacre, and Japan's postwar dependence on the United States. It tells of the inevitable rise of the dragon and its preparation for revenge. The song raps angrily that the two nuclear bombs dropped onto Japan are too light a punishment. It then speaks of the changing battlefield from military to "culture." It urges the Chinese people to resist Japanese "garbage," such as Japanese companies and popular culture, and it equates Chinese youth who consume Japanese popular culture with traitors lacking historical consciousness.

It is difficult to assess the effects of internet anti-Japanism, given the form and structure of the technology itself. The examples cited above clearly link nationalism with play—gaming and rapping—while at the same time promoting a nationalistic agenda. Two trends are essential to the process of collective identification in China's cyberworld today: consumerism and nationalism (Qiu 2004: 114). The effectiveness of this "consumer nationalism" is extremely difficult to assess, given the form of its representation. What is clear, however, is that nationalism will continue to thrive (albeit with restrictions and limitations) on cyberspace because it is the only state-sanctioned ideology where emotions and passions are allowed to congeal, adapt, and dissipate. More importantly, as Tessa Morris-Suzuki (2005) has observed about historiography in the age of multimedia, the digital hypertext is excellently suited to present a linked collection of short statements, images, and clips expressing diverse perspectives on the same event. However, hypertext tends to fragment rather than synthesize, and it cannot be used to address wider conceptual questions raised by complicated histories of imperialism, colonialism, or conflict in general. Furthermore, as Slavoj Žižek (2006) has observed, in supposedly unadulterated and uninhibited cyberspace, the user can "freely" express his inadmissible impulses because the rules regulating "real-life" exchanges are temporarily suspended. Hence internet identity is not just an imaginary escape from real-life impotence. Instead, in the guise of a fiction, the truth about oneself is articulated. What pervades this cyberspace is a lingering uncertainty: "I can never be sure who they are: are they really the way they describe themselves, is there a 'real' person at all behind a screen persona, is the screen person a mask for a multiplicity of people, or am I simply dealing with a digitised entity which does not stand for any 'real' person?" Despite the pervasiveness of nationalist sentiment on the internet, it is difficult if not impossible to gauge its real effect, given the uncertain nature of the medium and its usage. What is crucial is the recognition that popular nationalism takes the form of anti-Japanism at this historical juncture.

I have argued that anti-Japanism in China represents multiple historical attempts to articulate China's relative position in East Asia vis-à-vis its changing relationship to Japan, the only non-Western (nonwhite) imperialist power. Anti-Japanism is thus less about Japan than about China's self-images in the contexts of its own positionality in the region and beyond. Through my analyses of the deployment of *"guizi"* as incendiary speech against the Japanese in four historical moments—declining imperium, high imperialism, socialist nation-building, and capitalist globalization—I argued that the meaning of *"guizi"* has shifted from an effort to distinguish Japanese militarism from Japanese people to blurring and conflating these two categories. New media technology such as the internet, I suggest, has created a new form of rising Chinese nationalist sentiment that is at the same time concrete and elusive, converging and dispersing. In the final section of the chapter and shifting the use of the "Japanese devils" invective to the Japanese themselves, I want to demonstrate the productive aspect of the epithet when it is used in a self-reflexive and critical manner.

Guizi in Chinese Justice and Japanese War Crimes

Matsui Minoru's acclaimed documentary *Riben Guizi* opens with scenes from the Yasukuni Shrine on an August 15 where two factions—military apologists and antiwar protesters—voicing their respective causes, clash with each other. Some veterans don their military outfits to commemorate their fallen colleagues while some right-wing activists interrupt and threaten the protestors, yelling at them to get out of Japan. As men and women collectedly ask for peace and reflection on Japan's war, ultranationalist groups became increasingly agitated and violent. Amid the chaos, one can hear a man pleading to the bullying mobs, "We are bereaved family; we are bereaved family!" With images of young people seemingly enjoying postwar prosperity and somber music in the background, the director makes his intention of the film known with the following superimposed words:

> Our fathers and grandfathers bore arms in the name of a holy war, in fact, a war of aggression. What did they do in that war? . . . Although

much has been said of how that war victimized the Japanese, there has only been silence and denial about how we victimized others. In remembering the war, it is easy to speak of our victimization but difficult to address our own aggression. Yet that aggression reveals the true face of war, exposing as it does the terrible weak natures of human beings. We give our truth to future generations so they are not condemned to repeat our transgressions.

The self-reflexive and critical position aside, perhaps what is most poignant and reverberant from the film is the simple question "What did they do in that war?" *Riben Guizi* then proceeds to record confessions of violence, brutality, rape, and other heinous crimes committed by fourteen former Japanese soldiers in northeastern China. These men are mostly now in their eighties and half a century removed from their war experience. Grayed but spirited, and while some appear emaciated, they do not resemble the "Japanese devils" of the usual Chinese representations. Much like Hannah Arendt's description of Adolf Eichmann, these men, in their civilian attires and familiar surroundings, represent the "banality of evil" (1963). Without much emotion, the men speak matter-of-factly about their experiences in the army and their personal and collective misdeeds: indiscriminate killing, beheadings, rapes, arson, human experiments for biological weapon development, and cannibalism. The perpetrators' forthright and solemn confessions also reveal the conditions that made their actions possible (or justifiable) in the first place: namely, the emperor system, the dehumanization of Chinese people, peer pressure, and insensitivity (even pleasure) toward violence.

The former imperial soldiers' accounts are interspersed with newspaper headlines, archival footage, and photographs. A female narrator describes the escalation of the Japanese invasion to the Chinese mainland, Japan's imperialist reach to Southeast Asia, all-out war with the United States and its allies, and, eventually, the dropping of the atomic bombs and Japan's surrender. The chronology of the war events is a familiar one. However, the veterans' detailed descriptions of atrocity answer that simple question, "What did they do in that war?" from the ground and at an interpersonal level largely neglected in postwar Japanese narratives. It is only toward the end of the film that we come to understand the background and motivation of these men's confessions, which also constitutes the most controversial aspect of the film that, in turn, risks undermining the political mission the film set out to accomplish. As the narrator chronicles the dropping of the atomic bombs and Japan's surrender, we learn the plight of the estimated 575,000 Japanese soldiers who were in China at the time. They were subsequently interned in Siberia by the Soviets and assigned to hard labor. While there, 55,000 died without repatriation. In July 1950, the Soviets turned over 969 of the Japanese soldiers in Siberia to the People's Republic of China as anti-Chinese war criminals. They were held in the War Criminals Management Center in Fushun, Liaoning Province. Another 140 Japanese soldiers, who stayed on after the defeat and joined the nationalist fight against the Communists in Shanxi were confined under the Shanxi War Criminal Administration in Taiyuan. The fourteen witnesses in *Riben Guizi*, we are told, were among those held in those facilities.

We are then presented with footage of the prisoners of war being treated with medical care, given ample food supplies, doing physical exercises, and enjoying cultural activities. The narrator underscores the humanitarian treatment of the former soldiers by their detainers as directed by Premier Zhou Enlai and the Chinese Communist Party (CCP). In the footage, we see these Japanese soldiers eat, bathe, play, laugh, and live, albeit within the confines of the detention center. Gradually, the narrator tells us, the merciful care of the CCP has profoundly moved the criminals, and they began to feel remorseful for their wartime conduct. Many began to acknowledge their crimes during the occupation and to write apologies to the Chinese people. To culminate their transformation from "devils to men" (Kushner 2006), in June 1956, after six years of confinement in China, a Special Military Tribunal was convened under the Supreme Court of the People's Republic. Of the 1,062 Japanese held, and excluding those who died or committed suicide, only 45 were indicted. The rest were repatriated immediately after the trials.

During the tribunal, we see the former soldiers confess in detail their crimes, and then, when confronted by their victims' scarred bodies, began to break down and cry. While we do not hear the voices of the Chinese survivors, their anger and emotion, not to mention their bodily injury, are clearly visible, both to the perpetrators and to the film viewers. However, since only the victimizers' voices are audible and they are superimposed on top of the images of them crying and confessing, the film is devoid of the sentimentality and emotion that are usually associated with such confrontations. Those indicted were sentenced to eight to twenty years, but most were released before serving their full terms. Between June and August 1956, all the prisoners were released and repatriated to Japan.

The Japan that these soldiers returned to was unlike the Japan that they left. The narrator describes 1956 as the end of the "postwar" and signaling the dawn of Japan's "economic miracle" in the following decades. With rising national confidence and a diminishing consciousness of Japan's war in Asia, the returnees were met with suspicions of brainwashing and ideological conversion at the hands of the Communists. With the escalating Cold War, many former soldiers were placed under police surveillance and encountered difficulty and endured taunts as they searched futilely for jobs, not to mention marriage. The film ends with some of the soldiers expressing their conviction to break the silence in Japan about its war atrocities, especially for the younger generations so they would not repeat the horror of war in order to atone for their elders' crimes.

The fact that these men were interned at Chinese facilities, publicly acknowledged if not lauded, and granted such humane treatment only cast doubts on the "authenticity" of their testimonies. The nationalists predictably refuted their confessions as brainwashing and falsehood; even the liberals and sympathizers remain cautious. That all testimonies, whether by victims or victimizers, are viewed with various levels of suspicion is nothing new. The meticulous and repetitive accounts shared by the former "comfort women" of Korea (see chapter 3) are attempts to authenticate their collective experiences and also provide irrefutable facts about their abuse and suffering. There is no doubt that the Communists' benevolent forgiveness is conditioned on a political calculus to achieve favorable public relations. However, this does not preclude the fact that violent acts were afflicted on the Chinese population by these repentant soldiers. That their confessions are uncomfortable or seem improbable to postwar Japanese speaks volumes about the lack of deimperialization and the swift "rehabilitation" to democracy and demilitarization under Cold War American hegemony. Putting aside the veracity of the confessions for the moment, we need to ask the obvious questions: Why did the Chinese Communists treat the Japanese POWs humanely instead of seeking revenge? What was the Communists' motivation to conduct war-crime trials but then subsequently release all the Japanese soldiers? By examining the historical background of the tribunals of Japanese war crimes in China, we can better understand the impact of the emerging Cold War structure in East Asia and the impetus behind the trials and the Japanese soldiers' subsequent testimonies. My argument is that even if the veterans' confessions were conditioned by larger historical and political demands, their voices must still be heard and reflected on, especially amid the growing militant and nationalistic tension between Japan and mainland China today.

In his pertinently titled *Men to Devils, Devils to Men: Japanese War Crimes and Chinese Justice* (2015), Barak Kushner provides a detailed and comprehensive analysis of postwar legal maneuvers in the Chinese context to bring Japanese imperial behaviors to justice. To Carol Gluck's four terrains of memory—official commemoration in public monuments and school texts, vernacular memory in film and literature, personal memories, and public debates about memory—Kushner adds a fifth: legal or institutional memory. Legal memory is important, Kushner argues, because "it has a particular and binding hold on the future—such as peace treaties, court cases, lawsuits, legal precedents, and so on." Furthermore, "Legal memory is recorded in courts, used as the basis for international relations, and therefore forms a cornerstone for decisions that affect foreign policy. The linkage of these elements with international law makes their impact more valuable" (2015: loc. 488 of 8886). Kushner therefore grasps the Chinese trials from the outset as a transnational performance whereby the new People's Republic attempts to insert itself onto the postwar world scene via international law. Showing the world the benevolent Communist justice toward Japanese war criminals had become an integral part of the CCP propaganda campaign to seduce Japan to turn its back on U.S. support.

Even if we accept the Fushun trials as Communist propaganda, the importance of the Chinese trials is that they offered a de-Westernizing critique of the trials in Tokyo. Kushner contrasts the West-centric Tokyo Trial with the Communist trials in 1956. He writes:

> The Tokyo Trial pivoted on crimes against peace, A class crimes, so conventional war crimes and crimes against humanity did not gain public attention. The entire legal focal point was the start of the war or the debate about wartime responsibility and the policies that continued the war. As such, the International Military Tribunal for the Far East was essentially a politically oriented discussion, though not without merit, and therefore arguments about wartime atrocities or brutal military behavior mostly fell outside the confines of the

narrative and until recently stood beyond the historical pale as well. (2015: loc. 5620–25 of 8886)

In other words, the Chinese trials, by focusing on the Class B and C crimes, stood in contrast with the Western (American) victor's justice, and they were able to confront Japanese wartime violence against Chinese civilians, something that the Tokyo trials largely ignored. By exempting Emperor Hirohito from the trial and focusing on a few Class A war criminals, postwar Japan and its American overlord abrogated themselves from their respective war crimes in Asia.

The CCP's use of the trials as propaganda notwithstanding, the Chinese trials bring forward crucial contexts that were missing in the Military Tribunal for the Far East and in postwar Japan: the self-reflection of one's conduct and the confrontation by the surviving victims. The criminal trials in China have ironically emboldened the veterans to speak out openly. Linda Hoaglund speculates that one reason the former soldiers felt free to testify on camera is that, unlike most lower-ranking soldiers involved in Japanese war crimes, they had actually been tried, albeit in China, by a Special Military Tribunal and had already been confronted by their Chinese victims (2003: 9). Comparing it with the situation in postwar Germany, Hoaglund points out that since there is no statute of limitations for Nazi war crimes, if former Nazi come forward admitting their crimes, they would be incarcerated and prosecuted accordingly, regardless of their age or the distance from their crimes. The Japanese witnesses are legally exempt from prosecution and imprisonment and this, ironically, has enabled some to publicly testify against Japanese militarism and to admit their personal crimes (9).

It is instructive to compare the experiences of veterans who were detained in the former empire and those who returned and lived through postwar ruins and prosperity. Hara Kazuo's *The Emperor's Naked Army Marches On* (1987), for instance, chronicles the attempt by its main character, Okuzaki Kenzō, a former veteran, to track and confront his superiors about the unexplained deaths of his two comrades. Although the victims in this documentary are Japanese soldiers instead of Chinese civilians, what we see, besides Okuzaki's unusual methods of truth seeking and his propensity for violence, is the continued denial, deflection, and dismissal by those responsible for the heinous crime (cannibalism) against fellow soldiers. Okuzaki has to resort to unconventional ways to seek justice for his fellow soldiers because the Japanese government has never brought a single veteran to justice for war crimes.

Both Kushner and Hoaglund mention the friendships that were formed between the Japanese soldiers and their Chinese wardens even after their repatriation. The short-lived China Returnees' Association, or *Chūkiren* (1956–2002), provided a platform for the veterans to publish and speak out about their crimes so younger generations would not repeat the same mistakes. Kushner's legal memory of the Chinese trial and Hoaglund's contextualization of perpetrators' testimony amid postwar Japan's imperial amnesia shift the conversation of brainwashing and propaganda of *Riben Guizi* to questions of redemption, reconciliation, forgiveness, and healing. Lisa Yoneyama further argues for the "unintended consequence" of the Chinese policy and the experiences of the returnees from the normative procedure of justice and reconciliation. She writes:

> The Chūkiren members' contrition was born out of their face-to-face encounter with the immensity and sheer irreparability of the loss they inflicted on their wartime enemy Other. In their self-learning, the Japanese were the unforgivable; the Japanese war crimes were beyond repair. To them, the clemency did not mean the victims had forgiven them; it meant simply that the Japanese violators were free to live as the *forever unforgiven*. Instead of demanding that the victim enter the horizon of reconciliation and the economy of forgiveness, the practice of self-reckoning has established a radical incommensurability—hence unconditional fraternity—between the violated and the violator. It created an enigma, Derrida's "insoluble," that would forever sever the Japanese POWs from the state propaganda's intended dialectics. (2016: 134)

It is this "unconditional fraternity" that, to paraphrase Kushner again, allows for the Japanese devils to become human, once again.

THREE. Shameful Bodies, Bodily Shame:
"Comfort Women" and Anti-Japanism in South Korea

A Preamble

Writing about the "comfort women" is not easy for me. In March 2007, I was asked to serve on a panel when a student group invited a former comfort woman, Ms. Kim Ok Sun, to speak at the university where I taught. Ms. Kim gave her testimony, often pausing in tears. Afterward, my co-panelist talked at length on human rights. When it was my turn to speak, I felt extremely uncomfortable, if not a little incensed. I was angry at the self-absorbed and over-privileged students who used the occasion to flaunt their unreflexive self-righteousness and moral superiority; I was irritated at my colleague's (unintended) patronizing and universalizing attitude that subsumed Ms. Kim's experience under a discourse of human rights, with little regard or sensitivity toward Ms. Kim who, I surmise, must have repeated the same testimony and relived the horrendous experience countless times. Like Dai Sil Kim-Gibson, I had wanted to ask her what her life was like before her abduction, what were the happier times of her life (Kim-Gibson 1997: 255). Instead, I recounted the irony and imperialist traces that allowed me to speak to her only in the Japanese language a few minutes before the start of the event. Generations and continents apart, the only possible means of communication between Ms. Kim and I was within the imperialist language that had commanded her to become a sexual slave.

Personal experience aside, the difficulty of writing on the comfort women issue lies in the tension between the search for the historical veracity that would expose Japanese imperial violence and that would justify the demands for apologies and compensation, and the propensity to marginalize the women themselves as victims or witnesses only, which they have internalized to speak in public because that is the only discourse and avenue of appeal available to them. Paraphrasing Rey Chow, the comfort women must be sacrificed through their victimhood (2012: 86). It is in this context that the decade-old documentary trilogy by Byun Young-Joo remains one of the most intriguing studies of the lives of the comfort women. Unlike the normative documentaries on this issue, the trilogy is completely devoid of the historical footage that is customarily used to provide realism. Instead, Byun's films follow a group of women, chronicling their daily activities, which include attending weekly Wednesday protests. The films use interviews as a way to have the women talk about their experiences, during both their enslavement and their postliberation travails. As the films progress, the hard distinction between the filmmaker and her subjects begins to fade. Not only are the women beginning to become aware of being filmed, but they also actively engage with the camera. In *My Own Breathing*, a former comfort woman, Lee Young Soo—for most of the film—takes over for the director; she travels and interviews other former comfort women. The lack of sensationalism and sentimentalism allows the films to exhibit a raw sensibility that, ironically, makes the films more real, and it humanizes the women in their complexity and complicity, including their struggles for recognition, redress, and reparation. Before moving to analyze the issues of shame and the body in Byun's trilogy, it is useful to consider the dominant affect of *han*, a supposedly culturalist sentiment particular to the Korean people that laments the tumultuous history of Korea at the same time as it champions the Korean people's resilience.

Extreme Nationalism and Its Discontents

Consider these two following acts of anti-Japanism in South Korea.

On August 13, 2001, twenty young Korean men chopped off the tips of their little fingers while shouting "Apologize, apologize!" in their anti-Japan demonstration in the drenching rain in front of Independence Gate, which was once a prison that held freedom fighters during Japanese colonial rule. The enraged young men were protesting Japanese Prime Minister Koizumi Jun'ichirō's planned visit to the controversial Yasukuni Shrine to honor Japan's war dead.

On March 15, 2005, Park Kyung-Ja, a sixty-seven-year-old woman with weed clippers, and Cho Seung-kyu, a forty-year-old man with a knife, chopped off a finger each during a rally at the Japanese embassy in Seoul to protest Tokyo's claims on a group of desolate but disputed islands that the Koreans and Japanese call Dokdo and Takeshima, respectively.

Other forms of anti-Japan protest have included self-immolation, covering one's body with 260,000 bees, and decapitating pheasants in front of the Japanese embassy. These acts of extreme (as opposed to banal) nationalism (Billig 1995) violently perform Koreans' deep-seated indignation and trauma from thirty-five years of Japanese colonial rule on the peninsula, Japan's subsequent whitewashing and denial of war responsibilities, and the damaging legacies of colonialism. The symbolic meaning of severing fingers aside, these acts of mutilation, as emotive expressions, require us to consider the lasting antipathy toward "Japan" in the postcolonial present. While some women do participate in fanatical acts of protest, it is perhaps best to describe these performances as "masculine" or "hypermasculine." That nationalism has always been a gendered discourse is not surprising, especially among formerly colonized peoples, because the tropes of imperialist violence and its resistance are often constructed along gendered lines, and violence against women is enacted and utilized to humiliate the masculine foe. In this regard, extreme (or hyper) masculine anti-Japan nationalism, despite its symbolic and performative gesture, ultimately remains complicit with Japanese imperialism. Anti-Japanism, as long as it remains monolithic and directed externally as only a catharsis to overcompensate for colonial wounds, obscures its own internal violence and contradictions in the name of the patriarchal nation. One of the most publicized and yet unresolved issues of Japan–South Korea masculine connivances is arguably the comfort women case.[1]

Although the exact number is still in dispute, it is estimated that tens or hundreds of thousands of young women from various countries (but 80–90 percent from Korea) were abducted, raped, and mobilized by the Japanese Imperial Army to serve as sexual slaves at various "comfort stations" within the empire from 1932 to 1945.[2] The women's testimony and historical documents have shown that, during their internment, they suffered multiple incidences of psychological and physical torture and abuse. They were expected to "service" between ten and twenty men a day without compensation or proper medical care. It is estimated that 70 percent of these women perished before the end of the war, and a large number of them never repatriated. Even those who survived and returned to Korea after "liberation" could not return to their "normal" lives, because physical ailments due to sexually transmitted diseases and bodily abuse were compounded by severe psychological and emotional traumas. Shame and guilt elicited by strict Confucian codes of sexuality forced the women to remain silent so as to not become the pariahs of the postindependent, economically driven, and militarily ruled authoritarian postwar South Korean regime. The silence was finally broken on August 4, 1991, when Kim Hak-soon—with the support of feminist groups, religious associations, and other civic organizations—publicly recounted her ordeal as a military sex slave.

For postwar postliberation Japan and Korea, enclosed within the Cold War structure, engulfed in the hot wars in Vietnam and on the Korean Peninsula, the comfort women issue was all but forgotten if not repressed and acquiesced to in the face of the demands arising from the capitalist reorganization of the region. When, after Kim's public testimony, the issue gained international attention in the early 1990s, the Japanese government denied any wrongdoing and cited the 1965 Treaty on Basic Relations between Japan and the Republic of Korea, which established normal diplomatic relations between the two countries, as having already completed all colonial compensations to the Republic of Korea. The South Korean government also agreed to renounce any further demands for reparations.[3] This justification, which persists in official discourse even today, ignores the facts that not only was the comfort women issue suppressed if not censored in the 1960s, but also a crime against humanity cannot simply be offset by diplomatic negotiations. In 2005, the South Korean government disclosed 1,200 pages of diplomatic documents, which had been kept secret for forty years, revealing that the South Korean government had agreed to demand no further compensation, either at the governmental or individual level, after receiving $800 million in grants and soft loans from Japan as recompense for Japan's colonial rule from 1910 to 1945.[4]

The agreement between the two nations that supposedly reconciled the colonial question needs to be contextualized in the postwar Cold War capitalist reorganization in the region that required adherence to an American policy of developmentalism and anti-Communism. In South Korea, the "compressed modernization" under military authoritarianism has had dire consequences for the underclass, women, the undereducated, and the elderly. Although diplomatic goodwill cannot erase the people's traumatic memories of colonial rule and imperialist violence, the state, in its single-minded and class-privileged economic development, tried to mobilize anti-Japanese sentiments to achieve its own version of a masculine nationalism that would suppress internal difference and obscure contradictions associated with its policies (Cho 2001). The comfort women issue, therefore, is a three-layered story about war, gendered violence against women, and racialized violence visited mostly on Asian women, primarily those from impoverished, uneducated families. In this regard, race (imperialism), class (capitalism), and gender (sexism) intertwine in a complicated yet definitive way. However, as long as nationalism is the sole agent and arbiter for an anticolonial, anti-imperialist impulse, its homogenizing forces will only suppress questions of gender (patriarchy) and class difference (capitalism). It is within this "patriarchal colonial capitalism" that the comfort women issue must be contextualized. Chunghee Sarah Soh puts it brilliantly:

> Korea's comfort women embody this in the context of patriarchal colonial capitalism. Structural violence emanates from the economic, political, and cultural forces that are embedded in everyday life—notably gender, class, racial and ethnic inequality, and power imbalances. It is manifested in the abusive or demeaning exercise of power customarily practiced with impunity by one category of social actors or groups against others in situations of hierarchically organized social relations. Korea's comfort women were thus victims of the mutually reinforcing convergence of sexism, classism, racism, colonialism, militarism, and capitalist imperialism. (2008: xiii)

The "coming out" of the former comfort women in December 1991 signaled the coming of the post–Cold War era in East Asia, at least in terms of the suppression of the interrogation of Japanese colonialism and imperialist violence under American hegemony and Japan's complicity in the Cold War structure.

In this chapter, I analyze Byun's trilogy about the comfort women—*The Murmuring* (1995), *Habitual Sadness* (1997), and *My Own Breathing* (1999)—through the affect of shame and the trope of the body, arguably two of the most salient attributes of the comfort women's subjectivity. First, I argue that the socially imposed and gendered sentiment of "shame," in its conformity and acquiescence, allows the audience of these films to visualize the dilemma and the courage of these women in their decision to break their silence. Unlike the culturalist sentiment of *han* in Korean nationalist discourse, shame, or rather the overcoming of shame, has the potential to negotiate and move toward the politics of reconciliation, not with the Japanese nation-state (as it continues to deny the women's claims), but with family and loved ones. Second, if shame constitutes the most salient affective dimension of these women's existence, the aging body reminds us of the materiality of their suffering and the inevitable passage of time that further underscores the cruelty of postcolonial violence. Juxtaposing and associating the visibly aged women's bodies with that of Emperor Hirohito's dying and concealed body and the nationalized mourning surrounding his death, I argue not only that bodies are differentially valued and evaluated, but also that the cowardice of the imperial system once again abrogated the responsibility of the Showa emperor for Japanese imperialism and colonialism.

Han and Cultural Nationalism

Cultural nationalism has always been imbued with the politics of gender. Postwar postindependent South Korea is no exception. The imbrication between gender and cultural nationalism, I suggest, must be understood in the context of the "compressed modernity" of South Korea (and other late-industrializing states) in global capitalism, where a single-minded drive for economic development engenders an inequality and social contradiction that cultural nationalism tries to obfuscate or suppress. In the desire to "catch up" and modernize, South Korean society, with favorable capital flows and American Cold War policies, has embarked on a nationalist, developmentalist model that came crashing down during the International Monetary Fund (IMF) crisis in November 1997. As Cho Han Hae-joang has argued, the notions of *kukmin* (a member of a nation) and *kajok* (family) are two signifiers that have exerted the most power in the constitution of modern life in South Korea, a process that she refers to as "compressed colonial growth" (2001: 57). The demands for compressed development produced a society with only grand, state power and patriarchal families, but no citizens or autonomous individuals. In turn, the *kukmin*, along with *kajok*, made compressed growth possible. What is significant here is that in South Korea, as in many late-industrializing nations, nationalism is not contradictory to globalization. In fact, the concepts reinforce each other and are seen as constitutive, rather than antagonistic (Lee and Cho 2009). However, in times of crisis, such as the IMF bailout, nationalism is mobilized in order to save the nation.

Anti-Japanese sentiment and anti-Communism have been the driving forces behind Korean nationalism since liberation. In the so-called postcolonial, post–Cold War era, these antagonisms remain powerful sources of nationalist mobilization, depending on the desire and needs of the authoritarian developmentalist state during the Cold War and, more recently, the neoliberal developmentalist state under the regime of globalization. Historical colonial violence and contemporary economic severity have deprived Korean masculinity and patriarchy a sense of power, authority, and legitimization. In the colonial period, the father is stripped of his Confucian-derived power over the household and the nation, and he is rendered traditional and irrelevant in relation to colonially derived modernization and sciences. During compressed growth, the father is reduced to a financial provider, but at the same time he became the most instrumentalized and isolated member of the family. The crisis of masculinity, as many scholars have argued, manifests itself in the culture realm through what Kyung Hyun Kim has called "remasculinization" to cope with anxieties of humiliation and emasculation (Kim 2004).[5] In her critical assessment of work by the Korean auteur Im Kwon-Taek, Chungmoo Choi (2002) has powerfully demonstrated the structural similarity between Im's aestheticism and Korean cultural nationalism. More importantly, Choi argues that colonized Korean men attempted to respond to the deprivation of national identity and loss of masculinity by inflicting violence on colonized indigenous women or on the emasculated self. In *Sopyonjie* (1993), perhaps Im's most popular work, Yu-bong, the adopted father of Song-hwa, blinds her in order to deepen her *han*, the sentiment that one develops when one cannot or is not allowed to express feelings of oppression, alienation, or exploitation because one is trapped in an unequal power relationship. The feelings of anger, pain, sorrow, or resentment that find no expression turn into *han*. While *han* is purportedly a copious, collective, and shared Korean sentiment from its history of foreign oppressions and internal strife, it emerges at the intersection of two aspects of Korea's modern history: the inability to articulate the incommensurable experience of modernity, and the lament of the loss of an imagined secure past in the course of compressed modernization.[6] What is crucial here is that the bearer of *han* is the native woman. Choi writes:

The film adopts the viewpoint of both the colonial male gaze and the Othered feminine subject responding to that gaze. Under this self-primitivizing, internalized colonial male gaze, a daughter is blinded for perfection of a cultural nationalist artifact that fulfills the masculine desire of a father who has been shunted off to the margins of that capitalist development. The film attempts to sublimate the national *han* by recuperating a precolonial, aesthetic means of communication, *p'ansori*, as it highlights the *han* of a victimized woman who bears the burden of reclaiming national identity. . . . The victimized woman is given the role of the redeemer of the nation. (2002: 116)

Similar processes of recuperating masculinity and sublimating collective sentiment can be seen in popular films as well. Frances Gateward (2007) has suggested that three particular genres, the epic, the action film, and the sports film, with their continued invocation of the colonial past, work together to construct a collective Korean identity based on the normalizing of anti-Japanese images. Gateward situates these films that project anti-Japan sentiments within the crisis of masculinity over the advancement of gender equality and within the anxiety over the eclipsing of traditional gender roles. These "manly" genres collectively deny tropes of victimization. Gateward writes: "By revising the colonial past through a rejection of victimization, highlighting patriotism and nonpassivity, these films transform the traumatic social memory of defeat to one of active struggle. Integrated into the wider social context of increased nationalism, they serve as a kind of cultural glue for the 'imagined community,' aiding the creation of what the Popular Memory Group describes as 'dominant memory'" (205). It is in the context of "hypermasculinity" and its historical discourse that Gateward turns to Byun's three documentary films on the comfort women as critical and powerful interventions.

It is to Byun's work that I also turn in thinking about shame and the body as ways of confronting the historical injustice of sexual slavery and Japanese colonialism. As Gateward has pointed out, Byun's trilogy comes out of a long tradition of progressive documentary making in South Korea that eschews sensationalism and the historical narrative common to films on the comfort women. I want to suggest that, unlike the pervasive and "nationalized" notion of *han*, these documentaries offer a keen insight into the notion of "shame" that is internalized by the former comfort women as structured by patriarchal and Confucian authority. While reflexive of patriarchal culture, women's shame—I argue—has the potential to redirect itself to critique the patriarchal nation.

Shame

As discussed earlier, the constitution and affirmation of *han* require the mutilation of the female body. Without suffering, there is no *han*, a supposedly collective Korean sentimentality. The residual and persistent existence of *han* among the former comfort women (as they do hold grudges and indignation against those who perpetrated violence against them) cannot be denied. Despite the pervasiveness of *han* in Korean culture and general association with women's suffering, Soh has argued that the *han*-filled testimonials of some surviving comfort women show paradoxically, in the context of modernizing Korea, their *han*. This derives in part from their exercising personal agency against domestic oppression, such as the prohibition of girls to receive an education. In some cases, it is the *han* the women harbored for not being able to receive an education and to craft a modern self that drove them to be deceived by the Korean brokers and Japanese military who promised them work and education (2008: 82–85). That said, it is the sense of shame, in its multiple Korean iterations and embodied in the patriarchal Confucian tradition, that immobilizes these women.[7] Here, shame obviously refers to the sense of embarrassment and indignity of being sexually violated, and, in one of the woman's words, "disfigured." However, it is the feeling of shame and the overcoming of it that allow the women to gain some sense of agency and dignity amid the double oppressiveness of nationalism and imperialism. What makes the comfort women issue a fundamentally colonial issue is the patriarchal understanding of men's and women's sexuality. This understanding then incriminates both Japanese and Korean patriarchalism for denying and hence reasserting the self-shaming mechanism that makes the victim apologize for herself (Yang 1997: 65–66).

Ruth Leys has argued that shame (and shamelessness) has displaced guilt as a dominant emotional reference in the West. In her meticulous evaluation of clinical and theoretical analyses of Holocaust survivors from the 1940s to the present, Leys points out that the reevaluation of shame, heretofore subordinated to guilt, is symptomatic of a larger shift away from Freudian psychoanalysis to new theories of affect that see shame as anti-intentionalist, built-in, and belonging with other inherited physiological systems of reaction that are inherently independent of any intentional object (Leys 2007: 125). It is not the purpose of this chapter to engage the debate over "the turn to affect" in the humanities and the social sciences and the "intentionalist vs. nonintentionalist" arguments.[8] Instead, I am interested in Leys's observation that shame concerns aspects of selfhood that are imagined to be amenable to correction or change, whereas guilt is in principle irreversible, or at least not expungable. Eve Sedgwick has argued that "shame is simply the first, and remains a permanent, structuring fact of identity" for certain queer people (quoted in Leys 2007: 129). It is no different for the comfort women in their already having been exposed to the gaze of some real or fantasized Other (Leys 2007: 130). However, I would disagree with the notion that affects are nonintentional states but autotelic (Leys 2007: 133). Given the social stigma attached to the comfort women and their internalization of neo-Confucian sexology, the shame experienced becomes the condition of their silence and denial. In this regard, the comfort women's experience is akin to that of rape victims whose shamefulness and guilt are invariably personal, familial, but also national. It is only through various contradictory processes of suppression and revelation, cognition and conversation, that the women can overcome the sense of shamefulness and confront the demons within themselves.

The Murmuring (1995) follows the daily activities of six former comfort women who live in the House of Sharing.[9] In one early scene, one of the women, Park Doo-ree, tells the filmmaker that going to the monthly demonstration is akin to physical exercise. Park Ok-Nyong, one of her housemates, disagrees. "It's so humiliating," she says. She mumbles a bit and casts her eyes downward. "My god," she continues, "I couldn't even tell my mother." When the director asks Park Ok-Nyong if she feels humiliated when she demonstrates, Park lowers her face, looks down, pretends to do something else, and mumbles, "I am, at times." The lowered face and downcast eyes are classic expressions of shame, indicating feelings of embarrassment and ignominy, a dishonorable secret that cannot be shared even with one's own mother. In a public demonstration scene soon after, the women are seen with supporters singing and giving inspirational speeches. As the camera shows close-ups of the women, they rarely look at the camera and instead glance away. However, as the film progresses, the women gain confidence; they become more comfortable with the eye of the camera as well. But at this earlier stage, the grandmas looked tired and fragile in contrast with the volunteers' youth and energy.

The feeling of shame is what prevented many women from coming forward to testify against the Japanese government. However, Kim Duk-yeong decided to break her silence as one of a few remaining "live witnesses" when the Japanese continued to deny historical facts. The horrid experience and the shame have also instilled self-hatred in some women. Park Doo-ree, for example, talks about wanting to end her life because she has become an "invalid," and that dying is the only purpose in her life because she has hated her life for so long.

The film crew also travels to Hubei, China, to film three former comfort women who did not repatriate to Korea after the war. When speaking with Ha Koona, who was seventeen when she was abducted, the director asks if Ha's decision not to return to Korea after the war has derived from shame. The director expresses her own feelings: "But if you had come home to Korea . . . even ashamed. . . . I wish you had returned." To these feelings of sympathy, Ha can only express, "I wanted to, but I was so ashamed that I was in such a terrible place. Why? It was a place of shame."[10] The place of shame obviously refers to the comfort station where women were forced to serve between ten to twenty men per day with little attendance to their health and general well-being. And, according to Confucian tradition in patriarchal Korea, the women are no longer "pure" because they were sexually violated, regardless of circumstances. Shame, therefore, not only is about not speaking out, but also is an impediment to returning "home." Besides Confucian and patriarchal regulation of chastity, shame is also inflicted on the women's body. Another woman in Hubei tells the story of her being cut open because her vagina was deemed too small to serve men. She refers to her genitalia as the "shameful part," and that it is "pitiful." As she speaks, she looks down and away from the camera while shedding tears.

Bodies Have Expiration Dates

Given the nature of this historical tragedy, Chungmoo Choi (2001) has argued that the women's corporeal experiences lie at the core of the comfort women issue. The pain has registered on their bodies and memories through repeated rapes, beatings, mutilations, and injections of arsphenamine and opium to ease both bodily and ontological pain (398). Moreover, Choi points out that precisely because the bodily experience of the comfort women is that of sexual violation, their experience directly assaults the masculine desire of the Korean nation to overcome the symbolic emasculation that Japanese colonialism has left on the Korean male psyche. As a result, women's subjectivities are elided doubly: first, by Confucian ideology that objectifies women as the property of men, and, second, by anticolonialist nationalism that equates the nation with women's bodies. What surrounds the comfort women issue then, Choi contends, is the metaphorization of women's experience within the masculinist nationalist discourse and the erasure of the pain of these women, hence also erasing their subjectivity.

It is important to underscore that the comfort women's bodies were used to protect the bodies of imperial soldiers from diseases and to prevent the production of hybrid children from this mutually contaminating intercourse. The Japanese military medically regulated and controlled Korean women's bodies by regularly sanitizing them.[11] Hence the women's bodies are not only incarcerated and raped, but also disciplined and medicated, causing profound and lasting illness and deterioration of their bodies. When Kim Hak-soon first testified in public in August 1991 about her experience as a sexual slave for the Japanese military, she was already sixty-eight years old. Kim died in December 1997. During the time frame that the trilogy covers, most of the women interviewed were in their late sixties and seventies. Several also perished while making the films, leaving their demands for redress and reparation unfulfilled. As is the case with all historical victims, time is of the essence, because bodies wither and perish. Their youthful bodies were violated, mutilated, and abandoned; their aged bodies, neglected, disregarded, and scorned.

The Murmuring ends with two still photos of young comfort women and a moving image of an older, eviscerated body. The first photograph shows three comfort women (more like young girls) sitting on what appear to be stretchers or makeshift beds. Two women share one stretcher on the right, and one woman straddles the stretcher while holding an unknown item in her hands. It appears to be summer: all the women in are in short-sleeved dresses and one places a towel on her head to shelter herself from the heat. There are two women on the right; one looks at the camera while the other looks away, almost trying not to be framed by the photographer. The single woman on the left looks directly at the camera, expressionless. The snapshot, presumably taken while the women are resting from "work," displays their youthful, albeit fatigued, bodies: the "daughters of Korea." The photograph conveys a sense of quotidianness, and the women's facial expressions exude indifference, or perhaps an emotionless indignation. What is hidden from the photographic moment is the horror that goes on unphotographed, undocumented, and untold, until recently.

A second photo shows four young women in a medium close-up. While three women on the right appear preoccupied with writing something in a notebook, the woman on the left, also with a towel over her head and her chin on her left hand, simply looks into the distance and away from the camera's gaze. Once again, one is struck by the youthfulness of the subjects, which belies the nightmarish circumstances they are being subjected to. The film then cuts to a scene displaying the body of an aging woman, purportedly a comfort woman.

The transition from the still photographs to the moving image of the body is striking, as we go from the innocent-looking youths, as if stuck in time, to the haunting image of a faceless woman baring her body to the film camera. The body, however, is not simply aged as indicated by its limp breasts, folds, and wrinkles. In the image, we glance at what looks like a scarred and burned hand. But more stunningly, we observe what seems like wrinkled skin in a spiral pattern going into the belly button, evidence of a postsurgery body mark. The camera lingers for a bit and then closes in on the wrinkles and the sagging breast, then toward the shoulder and arm marked by wrinkles and crinkled skin. The camera then pans around her body, revealing her slow breathing through the pulsation of her belly area, then focuses on her scarred arm before fading out.

This last scene powerfully captures the lost youth of the comfort women (frozen in time, lost forever in the still photograph) that was stolen by the Japanese imperialist state and their presently living (although barely) bodies, still pulsating despite the aged, tormented, scarred, and violated flesh. In exposing the body in its materiality, as an embodiment of the repressed history of violence inflicted on these women, the film reminds us of not only the biologism of the body (that we all get old) but also the violence engraved onto its physical being. The focus on the body also alerts us to the limited time in which these aging bodies can receive any apology and reparation. Borrowing Elaine Scarry's notion that "bodily pain has no object outside the boundaries of the body," Choi has powerfully argued against the coalescing of women's bodily pain into a remasculinized national shame that translates their bodily experiences into the discourse of anticolonial nationalism (2001: 398). The film, using still photographs and moving images, provides a powerful visual language that represents the pained and shamed body that otherwise would be unrepresentable within the dominant language of patriarchal nationalism.

What the violence of sexual slavery has inflicted on these women is not just the physical and psychological damage they have endured throughout their lives. What the photographs of youthfulness indirectly suggest is the lives that Japanese imperialism has deprived them of—violently interrupted lives and dreams unfulfilled, or what one comfort woman refers to as "stolen innocence."[12] What the aged body displays are the traces of violation and "postliberation" patriarchal violence, leaving most of these women so damaged they could not bear children. Many are dismissed by their husbands or divorced for being barren. The knots around the belly of the woman metaphorically suggest the impossibility of her giving life, an essential role for women in the patriarchal nationalist society of postcolonial Korea.

Given their advanced age, it is not surprising that besides testimonies, demonstrations, and chronicles of their daily lives, the films frequently dwell on the women's health, their dying bodies, and their deaths. After a brief explanation by Byun about her reasons for making the documentary, *The Murmuring* begins with the one-hundredth monthly Wednesday demonstration, which began in January 1992 in front of the Japanese embassy. Even in their defiant speeches to condemn those responsible, the women are keenly aware of their aging bodies and reiterate that, even after their demise, they expect their descendants to continue to denounce the people responsible for their tragedy.

In recounting their experiences, almost all the women speak of abduction, deception, rape, and serving multiple men—between ten and twenty— a day. They speak of physical pain from coerced penetration and being beaten for misbehaviors, and from the agony of contracting venereal diseases that made them barren. Hong Gang Lim (seventy-five at the time of filming), who remained in China after the war, recounts her experience of being mutilated to enlarge her genitalia because hers was too small. Kim Bun Sun, for instance, in *My Own Breathing*, tells her interviewer, Lee Young Soo, another former comfort woman, that "men kept coming," that she didn't even have time to get up, and that her body couldn't take it anymore. One against many; a singular body against a sea of other bodies. In *My Own Breathing*, Shim Dal Yeon (seventy-nine years old) describes her first rape by multiple soldiers in which her body ceases to feel pain.

She cannot remember the rest of the incident and how long she had to endure the swarming of men waiting in line. She does, however, recall that, when she woke up, there was blood all over. The smell of foreign bodies and semen mixed with her own blood disgusted her. It was so nauseating that she threw up and had a headache. The smell of bodies and bodily fluids—blood and semen in their unconsented and instrumentalized mixing—is the smell of violence, violation, and disgust. It overwhelms and suffocates when the body becomes numb and unresponsive. The experience leaves her mentally unstable. After "liberation," she became a cook at a temple because there was "no place for crazy people to go except temples." Even to this day, whenever she sees a woman holding a man's arm, she thinks to herself that that woman is crazy. She chuckles and says, "Sometimes it makes me laugh. I know. I am the one who is crazy."

If *The Murmuring* is about testimony and living, albeit precariously, *Habitual Sadness*, the second film of the trilogy, is about dying. Conscious of being the subject of the film and perhaps believing in the power of the camera to sustain her, Kang Duk-kyong (sixty-nine years old) says to the director, "Film me a lot while I am still alive." In the first film, we find the jovial and energetic Kang diagnosed with lung cancer and dying. She asks to be filmed to the end. As with most women, she recounts being raped by a truck driver in Japan before she even began to menstruate. She is then taken to the military sexual slave unit to engage in forced sex with Japanese soldiers. Her body is "sore every week." She says, "It was a terrible life. It went on for about a year."

Unlike documentaries that purport to be objective, *Habitual Sadness* is replete with interactions between the women and the director/cameraperson. The women are fully aware of their own objectification and consciously ask the director to film them in a premeditated and purposeful manner. For example, in a lighthearted moment when Kim and Park are carrying and dropping pumpkins, the director asks: "Why did you ask us to film you carrying these pumpkins?" The women respond because they grew them and wanted the crew to film the harvest. When the director implores the women to say how they would like to be seen in the film, the women answer humorously: "As someone who works like a cow!" Here, the emphasis on the laboring body is important although conveyed as a joke. As women who have worked hard all their lives, they continue to insist on being viewed as laboring bodies. With some of their fellow former comfort women incapacitated and dying, they want to prove to the world that they have been working hard as testimony to their resolve to continue the struggle for redress and reparation. They are not just old women waiting for handouts from the Japanese and Korean governments. By demanding to be filmed in this way, they use the medium to assert their subjectivity.[13] Similarly, the dying Kang sees the film as a medium for achieving their goals for redress and reparation. In her dying bed, clearly deteriorating, Kang tells the director: "I've been thinking about this film. Lots of people may come to see it. I will pray that everybody comes. I hope it'll get a lot of attention. It may move people to help us. That is my utmost wish." Despite her impending death, Kang is willful and defiant: "We grannies are very old. But we live together like a family. Japan, be warned. You thought we'd back down if you threw money at us. We can survive despite our pain. We are determined. We've demonstrated over two hundred times on every Wednesday. To the last woman. We'll fight you, Japanese. I want the world to know our fight. We won't die easily. We will live long. We're strong. Japan made us strong. We will become stronger. We will live longer." On February 2, 1997, Kang left this world, her wishes unfulfilled.

Imperial Body and Imperialized Bodies

Except for the attention paid by their comrades and supporters, the many deaths of the former comfort women went by without much notice. Their deaths only highlight the lack of time to right the wrongs inflicted on them by patriarchal imperialism and nationalism. Despite their old age, they died too soon. Their anonymous deaths contrast sharply with the single preeminent death of the one who is most responsible for the plight of the women: Emperor Hirohito. Hirohito died on January 7, 1989, two years before Kim Hak-soon's public testimony. Hirohito's death (and his un-expectedly long life and reign), unfortunately, vanquished any attempt to investigate the emperor's war responsibilities, including the institution-alization of military sexual slavery. In this regard, Hirohito too died too soon. What is important here is not so much the unpropitious timing of the many deaths and a single death; rather, it is their association, or the lack thereof, that brings to the fore the suffering of the many and the eva-sion of the one: the one who should bear responsibility for the many. While the women lived mostly in misery after the war, sequestered in shame and silence, Hirohito was rehabilitated as "human" (despite the inhumane acts conducted in his name) and came to symbolize the pacifist and economically oriented new Japan created by American-designed Cold War imperatives. As Norma Field has succinctly pointed out, "In the postwar years the demands first of survival and then of recovery, reinforced by American security interests in the wake of revolution in China and the outbreak of the Korean War, and later, the headiness of High Growth Economics all served to render the question of Hirohito's war guilt moot and eventually taboo" (1991: 183). As the sole surviving commander of the original Axis Powers (Mussolini was executed and Hitler committed suicide), Hirohito was transformed and rehabilitated in the postwar years from a god-emperor and commander-in-chief of Japanese militarism to a symbolic emperor and microbiologist. His unexpectedly long reign encompassed three dramatic events in modern Japanese history: Japanese imperialism, defeat, and postwar economic recovery.[14]

The comfort woman's body is not just a gendered body, but a colonial body as well. It is a body used as military supply, a resource to enable the Japanese victory (Yang 1997: 65). We must therefore also apprehend the comfort women's issue as a colonial issue: hence, the implication of the Showa emperor and patriarchy as embodiments of both imperialist and masculine violence. Unlike the many ordinary deaths of the comfort women, Hirohito's demise was extraordinary. The course of his illness was meticulously reported (e.g., the amount of blood transfused). Indeed, a new vocabulary pertaining only to the emperor was introduced to describe his conditions. After his death, media and other commercial outlets displayed self-censorship and restraint in order to demonstrate their respect for the emperor. Unlike Kang's demand to be filmed until her death, the Japanese media had no access to publish anything regarding Hirohito's dying body. Whereas we saw Kang, in her deathbed, still demanding apology and reparation, Hirohito's passing more or less eliminated any possibility of even an admission of guilt, not to mention an apology.

Hirohito's dying and death, ironically, raised once again the long-suppressed question of his wartime responsibility. In *In the Realm of a Dying Emperor: A Portrait of Japan at Century's End*, Norma Field eloquently weaves three stories of ordinary Japanese citizens who courageously defy the postwar imposition of the "chrysanthemum taboo" and silence on war guilt. Unlike Hirohito, the people in Field's book—a supermarket owner who burned the Japanese flag, a widow who lost a lawsuit refusing to let her dead husband in the Self-Defense Force be enshrined as a deity, and the Nagasaki major who spoke openly of Hirohito's war responsibilities—all confronted Japan's past history of imperialism and contested the postwar state's denial and whitewashing despite social ostracism and right-wing attacks against them. They are important voices, much like the comfort women's demand since the early 1990s, for exposing and confronting the contradiction between Japan's postwar claims of pacifism and prosperity and its wartime and colonial responsibilities. The former conveniently suppressed the latter.

In December 2000, a transnational collaboration among women's organizations established the Women's International War Crimes Tribunal in Tokyo, which drew several thousand participants. The tribunal was organized, not unlike the Chinese trials of the Japanese war crimes discussed in chapter 2, as a countermeasure to the International Military Tribunal for the Far East that failed to prosecute and punish those responsible for establishing the military comfort system or committing mass rape during the war. The Women's Tribunal made two significant findings. First, it recognized the Japanese military comfort system as an institution of slavery that violated antislavery conventions and international treaties of the time. Second, it established that Japanese women who had been licensed prostitutes before their conscription into the military comfort stations were also victims of crimes against humanity, thus embracing the common victimization between Japanese and other women under the Japanese military sexual slavery system. Perhaps more symbolically, the late Hirohito was found guilty a year later in a judgment given in The Hague.[15] Equally important, as Lisa Yoneyama (2016) has pointed out, the Women's Tribunal, despite its limitations and shortcomings, exposed the fallacy of earlier war crimes adjudication, mainly the Tokyo War Crimes Trial. Not only did the Women's Tribunal find that Hirohito was responsible and that the Japanese imperial army had violated international laws prohibiting slavery and forced prostitution, it also indicted the Allied powers for suppressing knowledge of the comfort women system. Finally, the Women's Tribunal challenged the normative concept of "humanity" when it prosecuted military violence committed against women in North and Southeast Asia as "crimes against humanity," whereas the Tokyo War Crimes Trial exclusively focused on Japanese crimes against Western men and women (126). What is most pertinent to the aspiration of my argument is Yoneyama's insistence on radical reconfiguration of knowledge production toward futurity. She writes:

For the tribunal findings to gain any significance, audiences had to realize that its justice could not be located in the present, in institutional realism or the status quo. Instead, its significance had to be sought in the future, as the yet unseen, born out of a transformed present. In other words, the Women's Tribunal historical efficacy will depend on whether and how those who respond to the survivors' testimonial accounts become transnationally and nationally engaged so as to intervene critically in long-inherited institutions and knowledge. (127)

Conclusion: A Bronze Statue and Transnationalism

On December 14, 2011, the former comfort women, along with hundreds of volunteers and supporters, marked their one thousandth Wednesday rally. At the demonstration, the Peace Monument, a 120-centimeter-high bronze statue of a seated, unsmiling young girl, was erected to symbolize all the victims and face the Japanese embassy. Next to the seated statue is an empty seat, inviting visitors to sit with the girl and gaze at the embassy with her. With her feet bare, her hands on her lap, the girl's steely eyes fix on the embassy across a narrow street in central Seoul. The gesture of looking reminds us of the beginning of *The Murmuring* on an equally frosty December morning more than sixteen years earlier. In the film, one woman asks the police guards to move so she can "see" the embassy gate. This "seeing" or "glaring" is not only a call to view the "symbol" or "substitute" of Japanese aggression, but also a demand to be seen by those responsible. To be able to see the embassy gate is to render visible at all times the symbol of Japanese oppression. It also turns a downcast gaze of shame into a defiant look of demand. The bronze statue of the girl in traditional attire represents, on the one hand, the young victims who were enslaved and, on the other, its materiality recalls and reenergizes the fierce demanding gaze of the elder comfort women. It creates a sense of permanency, or a continuous demonstration, from what inevitably will become the ultimate fate of all the aging women. The installment of the bronze statue was not without controversy. Just prior to President Lee Myung-bak's visit to Tokyo that weekend, the Japanese government's main spokesman, the chief cabinet secretary Fujiwara Osamu, called the installation of the statue "extremely regrettable" and said that his government would ask that it be removed.[16] During a session of the Japanese Diet, Prime Minister Noda, responding to a question by the lawmaker Yamatani Eriko from the conservative Liberal Democratic Party, said "comfort woman forced into sexual slavery" is "far from accurate."[17] Not surprisingly, the conservative faction of the Japanese society took this opportunity to denounce the women as liars and to oppose the erection of the statue. On June 2012, Suzuki Nobuyuki, a forty-seven-year-old former member of the Diet, along with another unidentified Japanese man, tied a 90-centimeter-long stake to the leg of the statue with a sign that said "Takeshima is Japanese territory." Takeshima, or Dokdo, as it is called in Korea, is a small island located on the East Sea that has become a symbol of territorial dispute between the two countries. Suzuki uploaded a video on YouTube and a blog of his planting the stake. He also called the Peace Monument a "prostitute statue." A month later, in retaliation for planting the wooden stake, a sixty-two-year-old Korean man rammed a small truck into the main gate of the Japanese embassy.

The controversy surrounding the Peace Monument commemorating the one thousandth weekly protest only serves to underscore the continued impasse and escalating conflict over the comfort women issue. The state-to-state diplomatic sparring and scuffles are obviously not the solution, as both states are complicit in ignoring and marginalizing the crimes inflicted on these women. The sparring only mobilizes support or demonizes the women's supporters for political gains. However, this is not to say that therefore the state is irrelevant. If only the state can wage war, then also only the state can bear the ultimate responsibility for redress and reparation. The private fund concocted by the Japanese government is a sham, because it excludes, if not exonerates, the Japanese state from any responsibilities for institutionalizing the comfort stations and enslaving young Korean women and others of different nationalities. Twenty-plus years of protests, demonstrations, testimonies, education, and other activities have raised national and transnational consciousness about the injustices that former comfort women have endured, and they also raised awareness about the violence against women and children during wartime in general.[18] As Nami Kim has written, years of protest also "exposed the limits of a nation-state that has sought to build a so-called fraternal community in Korea, contesting its limited notion of citizenship."[19] The transnational support for the comfort women issue can be seen in the worldwide solidarity and the simultaneous protests supporting and commemorating the one thousandth Wednesday demonstration.

In December 2015, the Japanese and South Korean governments reached an agreement to settle the comfort women issue. Both sides lauded the accord as "epoch-making" and reflected the sincerity of the Abe administration toward resolving the issue. The agreement was as follows: Japan will provide a one-time 1 billion yen grant ($8.3 million) to set up a fund for the comfort women, which will be administered by the South Korean government. Abe will apologize to the comfort women and accept responsibility for the issue.[20] South Korea will consider the issue "final and irreversible" once Japan fulfills its promise. Both governments will refrain from criticizing each other over the issue in the international community. Finally, the South Korean government will seek to work with organizations in resolving the issue of the Peace Monument.[21] The agreement between the two states only underscores the limit and failure of patriarchal nationalism and representative governments. None of the comfort women were informed about the agreement, and the patriarchal states also decided to speak for the victims without consultation, empathy, or self-criticism. These women had waited for more than seventy years for redress and reparation, and they are still the pawns of bilateral diplomacy. To paraphrase Jacques Derrida (2001), this amounts to a "conditional" reconciliation, where two patriarchal states negotiated and settled on the betterment of international relations rather than confronting the issues and resolving them legally and ethically. I will discuss the possibility of "reconciliation otherwise"—outside the purview of the state—in chapter 6.

The rather hastily conceived agreement, however, points to the shifting geopolitical configuration in the region. The rapprochement could be interpreted as an attempt by both states to develop a mutual defense to counter the rise of China. As Noah Feldman (2015) writes: "What motivates Abe is the quest to improve Japan's national security. China's military expansionism is the main cause. Almost equally important is an accompanying perception that the U.S. may not be the strong protector it has traditionally been. Would the U.S. go to war to defend Taiwan from China? If the answer is no, then why would the U.S. go to war to protect Japan or South Korea? If there's doubt about the U.S. commitment, Japan and Korea need each other." As I argued in the introduction, anti-Japanism (and its constitutive Other, pro-Japanism) and its management today must be understood within the context of anxiety over the rise of China.

It is important to consider the concern and unease that the Japanese government and right-wing groups expressed over the comfort women statue. What threat does the statue of a young girl pose to the Japanese, in order to elicit destruction attempts and with its removal implicitly included in the bilateral agreement? I would suggest it is the statue's representation and materiality that resonate with the comfort women's supporters and at the same time threaten the opponents. The sculptors (Kim Seo-kyung and Kim Eun-sung) who designed the statue had initially envisioned the statue to be an old woman in her eighties, the approximate age of the comfort women at the time, holding a rod chastising the Japanese. However, they decided on the image of a young girl, around fifteen or so, about the age when they were taken, to represent their voice. The design has several intended symbolisms: the girl is wearing Korean traditional clothing, the *hanbok*; her short and rough hair represents forced hair cutting by the Japanese soldiers; the tightly clenched fists suggest a strong will to fight against the Japanese government's continued denial; and the bird on her left shoulder is a link between the deceased comfort women and those who are still alive (Lee 2016). In this regard, the statue mediates between the past, the present, and the future. It represents a past that deprived the girls of unknown possibilities, a present struggle against patriarchal nationalism, and a future of continued demand for justice even after all the comfort women have perished. What renders the statue empathetic and also alarming to the supporters and naysayers, respectively, is her verisimilitude, that she is neither a statue nor a real person, but both at the same time. Thus, the statue also mediates between "real" life and "fantasy." It is therefore common to see people putting a hat on her head or a scarf around her neck to keep her warm from the wintry weather, or people placing a stuffed animal next to her to keep her company.

Other than representations, it is the materiality of the statue that grounds and begets an undeniable physicality to the comfort women issue. A sculpture, W. J. T. Mitchell has argued, "does not project a virtual space, opening a window into immensity as a landscape painting does; it takes up space, moves and occupies a site, obtruding on it or changing it" (2000: 166). The comfort women statue, by its sheer materiality, occupies a site, in this case in front of the Japanese embassy, that rallies the supporters of the comfort women and becomes an eyesore for the Japanese government. Furthermore, as the sculptors have created thirty statues of the comfort women thus far, its materiality is also reproducible and, more importantly, transportable, allowing the comfort women statues to be exhibited in memorial parks, museums, and streets in Korea, the United States, and Canada. Recent controversies over the comfort women statues in Sidney's inner west and California's Glendale Central Park between local Korean and Japanese communities only attest to the transnational movement of the comfort women issue and the tenacity of nationalist discourse in the era of globalism.

The empty seat next to the Peace Monument evokes the transnational, translocal possibilities of the comfort women issue. It is an open invitation for anyone who cares about justice, who opposes violence, and who is inspired and humbled by the continuous efforts of the women who not only survived horrendous lives as sexual slaves, but also endured in the conviction and hope that the issue of comfort women would be resolved one day.

In the 1990s, there were 234 Korean women willing to break decades of silence about their history as sex slaves. As of July 2017, only thirty-seven remained.

FOUR. Colonial Nostalgia or Postcolonial Anxiety:
The *Dōsan* Generation In-Between "Retrocession" and "Defeat"

Now that we were free, had subjugation ceased to exist?
Who would be our slaves? When we were colonial subjects,
we could dream of freedom, but now that we were free, what
would our dreams be? Were we even free?
—SADDAT HASAN MANTO, *Kingdom's End*

On the morning of June 7, 2007, Lee Teng-hui, the former president of Taiwan and self-proclaimed one-time Japanese subject, fulfilled one of his long-standing wishes and visited the Yasukuni Shrine. Lee insisted that he took the pilgrimage only to mourn his late brother, who perished fighting in the Japanese navy in 1945. Lee's brother, who died in the Philippines, was enshrined under his Japanese name, Iwasato Takenori. Just before going to the shrine and amidst a media blitz, Lee told reporters that it was a personal matter and asked them not to construe his visitation in any political or historical context. He added that since his father did not believe his older brother was killed, they still had no memorial tablet at home, nor had they held a memorial service on his brother's behalf. Lee's personal journey to the controversial shrine expectedly drew the ire of the Chinese government, which has long regarded Lee as promoting Taiwan independence and defying the one-China policy insisted on by the Communist state.

On September 17, 2007, South Korean's Truth and Reconciliation Commission published a report on 202 Koreans who had collaborated with the

Japanese between 1919 and 1937. Established in 2005 by "the special law on the investigation of collaborations for Japanese imperialism," the commission published 106 names in December 2007 for the period between 1904 and 1919. As stated on its official website, the commission's aim is to "reveal the actual state of collaborations done in the period of Japanese imperialism in Korea to ensure historical truth and national legitimacy and thereby to realize a just society." Furthermore, the commission is entrusted to embark on a historical mission to rectify the shameful history of Korea's colonial past in "preparing the start of a new national history at the beginning of the twenty-first century."[1]

For the history of Japanese colonialism in Korea, the contrast between these two events cannot be starker. It reaffirms the common perception that the Taiwanese are unilaterally pro-Japanese and that the Koreans are unequivocally anti-Japanese. For Lee, the visit to the shrine was a symbolic gesture (his disclaimer notwithstanding) to reconnect with Japanese rule and to reassert Taiwan's historical identification with Japan. For the commission, the investigation is to purge elements of Japanese rule and its symbolic collaborators from its national history and to reclaim Korea's autonomy from the memories of colonialism. In both cases, the personal and the national intertwine, but in diametrically opposing ways. Lee's brother, or more precisely his spirit as a former colonial subject, is resurrected as a mediating force that rekindles both familial and colonial relations, and this resurrection reconfirms Lee's and Taiwan's historical and emotional connectivity to Japan. (Lee claims he wasn't aware that his brother's spirit was enshrined in Yasukuni when he visited Japan as vice president in 1985.) The 1,005 "traitors" identified by the commission, with their individual names and crimes publicly displayed (some with their properties and assets posthumously confiscated), demonstrates the resolve of the state to punish those who conspired with the Japanese and to insist on a radical break from Korea's "shameful history."

It is not the purpose of this chapter to elaborate on the difference between Taiwan's pro-Japanism and Korean's anti-Japanism. Any comparative methodology based on a putative national frame is obviously inadequate to account for the myriad historical causes and contingencies in both pre- and postcolonial contexts.[2] Instead, I am interested in exploring the sentiment of nostalgia and intimacy toward Japanese colonialism as displayed by former colonial subjects such as Lee and the so-called Japanese-speaking tribe (*nihongo zoku*) of his generation, or what the Japanese writer Shiba Ryōtarō affectionately referred to as the "old Taipeis" (*lao taibei*). What I want to suggest is that the favorable and at times intense feelings toward "Japan"—imagined or real—must be grasped as a desire to recuperate a sense of loss in both personal and historical terms. With many of these men (and a few women) in their late seventies and early eighties, and as the last generation of Taiwanese who had significant contact with Japanese rule, they fear that their impending death will also mean the end of the historical linkage between Japan and Taiwan. From a regional perspective, their sense of loss is exacerbated by the real and perceived decline of Japan and the rise of China in East Asia. Their anxiety, I want to argue, is symptomatic of the larger historical shift in the region. The modern/colonial and postwar/Cold War systems in Asia characterized by the dominance of Japan appear to have come to an end. And these elderly Taiwanese's desires for reconnection and anxiety for Japan's regeneration are only its symptoms. Furthermore, I want to resist judging these aged but spirited voices as simply the nostalgic yearnings of the formerly colonized or as the illusory fantasies of the feeble-minded. Instead, I understand their passion as a belated plea for recognition from the former colonizers of their marginalized existence since the end of formal colonialism. Their efforts, despite the obvious pro-Japan sentiments, interrupt the linear narratives of (1) colonialism → retrocession → nation-building and (2) colonialism → war defeat → nation-building schematics espoused and expounded by the Kuomintang and the Japanese state, respectively.

The *Dōsan* Generation

Unlike the young consumers of the so-called Japan-fever tribe (*hari-zu*) in contemporary Taiwan, whose identification with Japan is exclusively driven by consumption, the older generation's relation to Japan is mediated through recollections of belonging, social order, and the lament of being abandoned. As mentioned earlier, there are a couple of terms used to refer to this generation of pro-Japanese Taiwanese: the "Japanese-speaking tribe" (*nihongo-zoku*) or "old Taipeis" (*lao-taibei*). However, I would like to use the personable and Taiwanized term "*dōsan*" to describe them. The word "*dōsan*" derives from the Japanese "*tōsan*," meaning father. "*Dōsan*" has enjoyed some currency in (post)colonial Taiwan among Taiwanese-speaking families and conveys an amicable and respectful sentiment. The slippage from the original "*tōsan*" to the bastardized "*dōsan*" signifies not only the traces of colonialism but also the process of acculturation and appropriation. In 1994, Wu Nien-Jen's *Duo sang/Dōsan* (A borrowed life), a film based on Wu's father's life living through Japanese and nationalist regimes, gained critical attention and brought the term into popular and public consciousness. "*Dōsan*" therefore refers to the generation of men who spent their formative years under Japanese rule and were traumatized by the ensuing recolonization by the Kuomintang (KMT). After years of living in relative quietude under the KMT's anti-Japan policy and authoritarian regime, the *dōsan* generation only recently began to publicly express their thoughts in their memoirs. As depicted in the film, *dōsan* exudes a sense of masculine dignity, sadness, and loneliness from the alienation he suffers under the new regime and from his longing for a Japan that is no longer in his "borrowed life." Largely because of their explicit pro-Japanese sentiment and their seemingly anachronistic existence in contemporary Taiwan, the *dōsan* generation has found sympathetic ears among Japanese neoconservatives. More often than not, the Taiwanese are being propped up by the Japanese as simply confirming the conservative and nationalist agenda. The complicated and contradictory emotions and sentiments effected by the historical shift from colonial to (post)colonial conditions and Japan's "responsibility" toward these former subjects are rarely mentioned or interrogated. Their "Otherness" is again being assimilated into a "Japaneseness" that they can never possess but can only lament at its alleged passing, much like their own tumultuous lives.[3]

The complicity between the *dōsan* generation and Japanese neoconservatives is neither new nor surprising. As Mori Yoshio (2001) has argued, several former advocates of Taiwan independence residing in Japan, such as Huang Wen-hsiung and Jing Mei-ling, have switched from their earlier critique of Japanese rule to become the spokespersons for the Japanese neoconservative agenda. This radical turnaround, Mori suggests, is largely due to the political democratization of Taiwan since the 1990s, which increasingly diminished the relevance of Japan-residing pro-independence advocates. The conservative turn was induced by a number of political failures and the *dōsan* generation's own sense of irrelevance, not to mention the need to rationalize their struggle for Taiwan's independence and their existence outside of the island-state. The desire to be heard hence pushed them toward a mutual utilitarianism with Japanese neoconservatives. More important and instructive here is Mori's harsh indictment of postwar Japanese leftists' indifference to and ignorance of the voices of the formerly colonized. Progressive and leftist intellectuals, Mori argues, in their postwar political correctness, have bought into the "pro-Japan Taiwan" and "anti-Japan China/Korea" binary structure of the Cold War. Since Taiwan under Chiang Kai-shek's rule was ostensibly a client state of the United States, it automatically meant all voices from Taiwan are anti-Communist and hence nonprogressive. Mori points out that this radicalism actually concealed the arrogance of the former Japanese colonizer in its refusal to actually confront its own colonial history. The inattentiveness and marginalization of Taiwan by the Japanese leftists ironically obscured the colonial connection between Japan and Taiwan in the postwar years. Furthermore, the Japanese government acquiesced to the authoritarian Chiang regime by forcefully repatriating pro-Taiwan independence student leaders residing in Japan in the 1970s so that they could be prosecuted upon their return.

Nihonjinron from Taiwan

The texts that I have chosen for this chapter can be categorized under the larger rubric of "Nihonjinron from Taiwan"—writings on Japan and the Japanese in the (post)colonial era. This corpus of works can be classified under the following categories: (1) periodization—from postwar to the end of martial law (1945–87) and from post–martial law to the present; (2) authorship—texts written by the so-called *waishengren* (mainlanders and their descendants) or *benshengren* (native Taiwanese); and (3) languages—those written in Chinese or Japanese.[4]

According to a study by Huang Chih-huei (2004), between 1947 and 2000 approximately forty books were published in the Chinese language, with the majority coming only after 1987. In the immediate postwar years, as is to be expected, books on Japan were mostly written by *waishengren* from the perspective of a victor nation. Even if they were written by *benshengren*, they were published only with the tacit approval of the *waishengren* ruling party and they reflected the approved political view of the KMT. Sentiments about personal relations between the former colonizer and the colonized are subsumed and silenced under the binary between the "victor" and "loser" nations, the heroic anti-imperialists and the evil colonizers. In short, during this period, Chinese-language writings on Japan reflected a *waishengren's* perspective as "invaded peoples" (as opposed to a *benshengren* perspective as "colonized" peoples). The *waishengren's* is the perspective concurrent with anti-Japanism on the mainland during the war of resistance. The subtle but unmistakable distinction between "invaded peoples" and "colonized peoples" is important, for it not only marginalized the experience and perspective of the native Taiwanese, but also rendered colonialism invisible in postwar nationalist discourse.

In the post–martial law era, writing about Japan from the perspective of the formerly colonized flourished, especially from the 1990s onward. Twenty-four Taiwanese Nihonjinron books were published between 1992 and 2003. These works were mostly written in Japanese by *benshengren* and were either self-published or published in Japan. Most of these were penned by nonprofessional writers and employed mostly the literary forms of biography, memoir, autobiography, and poetry. These works recollect and reexamine with immense emotion and conviction personal experiences ranging from ardent condemnation of Japanese rule to equally passionate affirmation of Japanese colonialism. The shift from the perspective of the "invaded" to that of the "colonized," propelled by the democratic movement in Taiwan since the 1990s, opened up a new space for a more Taiwan-centric understanding of its own history, especially in the colonial period.

I have chosen for analysis four recent works that follow the Taiwanese/colonized viewpoint expressing profound nostalgia and fondness for Japanese colonialism. This choice is not entirely arbitrary. First, these works were all published in Japanese within a book series entitled "Pride of the Japanese" by Sakuranohana Publishing House, a small publisher that obviously harbors a neoconservative and neonationalist agenda.[5] The series title seems to elicit a double reading of "Japanese": those former subjects who are proud of once being Japanese, and Japanese today who are being called forth to be proud of their country. Second, these texts share, if not dutifully expound on, the rhetoric and discourse of neoconservatives such as Ishihara Shintarō and Kobayashi Yoshinori. The facile thing to do would be to assume that these "Pride of the Japanese" authors are nothing but dummies spewing the words of their Japanese ventriloquists. However, I would like to argue, in the context of (post)colonial Taiwan/Japan/China, that their discourse of nostalgia has to be apprehended as a rupture from the linearity of historical progress from colonialism to recovery and finally to nation-building. By equating their voices with simply conservative and reactionary gibberish by people in the twilight of their lives is to reproduce the colonial violence that constructed their subjectivity in the first place. It is also to flatten out the ambivalence of colonial power and the false faith in "liberation." The nostalgic mode of their writing forces us to confront a violence that continues from the colonial past into the (post)colonial present.

"Pride of the Japanese"

In the context of South Korea's investigation into former collaborators with the Japanese, the *dōsan* generation appears to be worse than "traitors," because they openly praise Japanese rule.[6] The series "Pride of the Japanese" has published four books since 2003: *Nihonjin wa totemo subarashikatta* (The Japanese were wonderful) by Yang Suqiu/Yō Soshū (2003), *Kaerazaru Nihonjin* (The unreturned Japanese) by Cai Minsan/Sai Binzō (2004), *Bokoku wa Nihon, Sokoku wa Taiwan: Aru Nihongozoku Taiwanjin* (Motherland is Japan, fatherland is Taiwan: A Taiwanese from the Japanese-speaking tribe) by Ke Desan/Ka Tokuzō (2005), and *Subarashikatta Nihon no sensei to sono kyōiku* (Wonderful! Japanese teachers and their education) by Yang Yingyin/Yō Ōgin (2006).[7] With Yang Suqiu/Yō Soshū as the sole woman, they all fit the profile of the *dōsan* generation: the authors were mostly born in the 1920s and 1930s and spent their formative years of schooling during the period of imperialization (*kōminka*) and war mobilization; they experienced the end of war during their youth and with a strong sense of confusion and depletion; they also lived through the rule of the "recovering" nationalist regime. When these books were published, their authors were already in their seventies and eighties. Before examining the formal structure of their writings—what I call the nostalgia mode—it is important to look at the role that these writings purported to serve under the series "Pride of the Japanese."[8]

According to the editor, the goal of the series is to explore and reconfirm the essence that forms the spirit of the Japanese at a time of the nation's uncertainty and instability. The story is a familiar one. The crisis of the nation, despite its relative economic wealth gained since the end of the Second World War, is that Japan and its people are not being respected by other nations. The examples of servile diplomacy toward China and North Korea and the controversy over the prime minister's visit to the Yasukuni Shrine all point to Japan's lack of sovereign power. The culprits, the editor insists, are postwar institutions such as the Japan Teachers' Union and left-leaning media such as the *Asahi Shimbun*. This "masochist view of history," as neoconservatives like to say, rendered Japanese colonialism as evil and invented war crimes beyond the normative violence of war. The fabrication of the Nanjing Massacre is its prime example. Contrary to these claims, the editor asserts, Japan modernized Taiwan and Korea with infrastructure-building, education, a sense of public duty, and legal institutions unlike the exploitative colonialism of the Western powers. These are claimed to be exemplary accomplishments that only the Japanese achieved.[9]

The "advancement" of Japan in Asia, accordingly, was not based on avarice but self-defense. While some ambition was involved, Japanese expansionism was vital to Japan's self-preservation and to securing the Greater East Asian Co-Prosperity Sphere from Western encroachment. While it would be wrong to praise all acts conducted by Japan, it is the goal of this series to "capture and rectify the historical truths that have been unjustly distorted." The editor then goes on to explain the different reactions to Japanese rule by the Taiwanese and the Koreans despite the mutual benefit of colonialism. As far as Taiwan is concerned, the oppression of the nationalist regime (as evident by the February 28 Incident, when native discontent and frustration about corruption, social disorder, military abuse, and economic hardship exploded in an islandwide protest against the nationalist regime) has further exploited and infuriated the people of Taiwan and made them long for their former ruler. Korea, by contrast, was blanketed by an anti-Japan regime under the watchful eye of the United States. The Korean nationalists, denying any contribution by Japan toward Korea's modernity, fabricated and brainwashed people for the last sixty years with their own national superiority and their belief in the inherent evilness of the Japanese.

The editor goes on to call for a racial and regional solidarity to oppose the continued Euro-American racism and hegemony in the world today. The series calls for the construction of and deepening of spiritual, economic, and political linkages among the yellow race nations to create civilization/culture that is distinct from that of Euro-America. This is the only way to reverse the long-standing tradition of white/Western envy of the Asians. As if to reconstitute the Co-Prosperity Sphere of the 1940s, Japan, Taiwan, China, Korea, Thailand, Myanmar, Indochina, Mongolia, Tibet, Bhutan, Nepal, and Sri Lanka—the Buddhist and Confucian cultures—must affirm their similar values. Only then can there be an Asian race worthy of the respect of the European race that has ruled much of modern human history. To illustrate Japan's "positive" colonial experience and its relevance today, the editor ends with words from the former Thai Prime Minister Kukrit Pramoj. Expressing his gratitude to Nakamura Aketo, the former Japanese military commander stationed in Thailand in 1955, Pramoj writes:

> Thanks to Japan, all Asian nations have gained independence. Japan, the mother, has had complications during this difficult birth. However, all the children are growing up quickly and healthily. Whom should we thank today that peoples of Southeast Asia can speak to the United States and England as equals? It is due to our mother, Japan, who sacrificed herself for the benefit of all. The eighth of December [the attack on Pearl Harbor] is the day mother revealed to us this important truth when she wagered her life on a critical decision. August fifteenth [Japan's surrender] is when our dear mother rested in her sick bed. We should never forget these two dates.[10]

The evocation of the old colonial East/West binary seems ludicrously outdated and ideologically suspicious in the context of today's capitalist globalization. It amounts to a feeble gesture to resuscitate the logic of regionalism under Japan's leadership. The former colonial subjects are ushered in as witnesses of Japan's colonial achievements and as advocates for the repressed truth, unspeakable in contemporary Japan, about its own past. The publisher intends to reconstitute the pride of being Japanese through the voices of formerly colonized subjects, and they seem happy to oblige. However, I want to suggest that, through the analysis of their nostalgia mode, the voices of those who once were Japanese cannot be so easily assimilated.

The Nostalgic Mode

Despite chronicling their individual life stories within the larger historicity of colonial/(post)colonial Japan and Taiwan, writings by the *dōsan* generation share a common narrative structure and rhetorical strategy that I have called the nostalgic mode. The nostalgic mode calls on us to view (post)coloniality in a particular sequence that corresponds to the lives of the *dōsan* generation. Personal experiences become testimonies to larger historical events, and historical events inform the trials and tribulations of individual lives: a dialecticism that underscores the connectivity and organicity between Taiwan and Japan. The nostalgic text usually begins with the author reflecting on an individual or a group of Japanese to whom the author either owed gratitude or with whom she or he shared fond memories. This "peaceful and stable time" was characterized by the presence of "kind and gentle policemen and soldiers" and "wonderful teachers." The text then recounts the numerous achievements of modernization that Japanese rule has accomplished in Taiwan, such as education, infrastructure-building, medicine, law and order, and so on. The benefit of Japanese colonialism is then followed and juxtaposed by the ruthless authoritarian rule of the KMT, usually highlighting the infamous February 28 Incident and the white terror era of the 1950s. The book generally ends with the author's opinion on and concern about the "degeneration" of the Japanese nation today, and he or she pleads for the Japanese to remember the historical connection between Japan and Taiwan and to be proud of Japan.

The titles of the books connote the sense of nostalgia, announcing a lament and fondness for a constructed past—*suteki datta* (it was wonderful), *subarashikatta* (it was marvelous). The authors often play the role of former Japanese subjects, much like adopted children who were left behind by Japan's defeat and repatriation. They are witnesses to the greatness and benevolence of Japanese colonialism, and reflect opinions and convictions that have been refuted and repressed in Japan since 1945. Their functions are thus liminal and surrogates—both inside and outside of Japan (as indicated by the translated titles "The Unreturned Japanese" and "Motherland Is Japan; Fatherland Is Taiwan")—for former Japanese; they can speak for the conscience of Japan that has been silenced in the postwar (post)colonial years.

Nostalgia has been a key concept in understanding postmodern aesthetics and politics under late capitalism (Jameson 1991). More specifically, it has been considered as the symptom or cause of the rift between historical signifiers and their signifieds. More often than not, nostalgia has become a term employed to accuse attachment to and affect for the past as being too politically reprehensible and empirically untenable. Both charges depend on a particular understanding of the proper way of relating to the past: it was only after history was understood as necessarily emancipatory, progressive, and rationally comprehensible that affect for the past could come to be condemned as an irrational obstacle. Those devoted to the past—or to that which becomes coded as the past—are seen as inhibiting history's progressive movement toward less exploitative modes of production (Natali 2004). The nostalgia expressed by the *dōsan* generation is indeed politically conservative and preserves class privilege. However, it is also a struggle for recognition from the former colonizers. In an unintended way, (post)colonial nostalgia fractures the ideology of historical progress from colonialism to postcolonialism, from liberation/ recovery to nation-building. It challenges the ideology that history is the narrative of progress toward an improved sate. Nostalgia is a symptom of the real unease caused by an unjust condition caused by the double artic- ulation of "liberation" and "defeat." The *dōsan* generation was caught in- between historical and political processes not of their choosing, and this confused them about the simultaneous "liberation" from the Japanese and "defeat" by the Chinese.

This nostalgia is about affect, and it is a sense of intimacy and senti- mentality that is corporeal. As Ke Desan writes about his relationship to Japan in an abstract, emotive way, "After all, I am nostalgic. Although it is only my personal opinion, my feelings toward Japan are not about like or dislike. I am nostalgic. It is probably something that has seeped deep into my body and soul that made me think this way" (2005: 232). But this sentiment also has its material conditions. Ke continues: "For example, I can't express myself without using Japanese. Although I use Taiwanese in my daily conversation, there are many expressions in Japanese that are missing in Taiwanese. When I read and write, it is mostly in Japanese. Mandarin Chinese is the third language I learned after the war. Compared to the young people, I am poor at it. It is a fact, however, through Japanese I have expanded my thinking and knowledge. It has been a plus to my personal growth" (232). Because Taiwanese is mainly a spoken language and Mandarin Chinese was imposed after "liberation," it is not surprising that Japanese, which he learned under the colonial education system, like most Taiwanese of his generation, defined and constructed his thoughts and worldview. It is precisely this colonial condition that Ke cannot on- tologically see himself ever separating from—the very condition of pos- sibility that defined his being in the world. He continues: "Today, even if I wanted to cut all my ties to something called Japan, I can't. It is because of the blessing of (Japan's) raising me and the nostalgia that remains with me. Japan has already become part of me. This is my conclusion" (233).

It is easy to either celebrate Ke's reflection as confirmation of the great- ness of the Japanese empire (the perspective of the neoconservatives) or to condemn it as a false consciousness of a "collaborator" (the perspective of the nationalists). Those two diametrically opposed readings are indeed possible, and they might seem to be the only ways these soliloquies can be read. However, I would argue for another possibility. The sentiment attached to the inseparability between Japan and its former colonial subject testifies to the repressed continuum of colonialism, in the form of a "distorted Japanese" in the (post)colonial present. What continues is not the same colonialism, but is the reflection of a forgotten and neglected former colonial subject reclaiming his subjectivity as having now been suffused with traces of an undeniable coloniality. It is a colonial difference that can neither be subsumed entirely under the category of "Japanese" nor can it be fully defined as "Taiwanese" or "Chinese."

"Japanese Spirit"

All these writers, when reflecting on what they missed most about the colonial period, unanimously point to the loss of the "Japanese spirit," not only in postwar (post)colonial Taiwan, but in contemporary Japan as well, and they express how the *dōsan* generation embodies and inherits this Japanese spirit. Kobayashi Yoshinori (2000) enthused in *Taiwan-ron* that the Japanese spirit, lost and forgotten in Japan, can only be found in Taiwan. It is important to understand, however, that the notion of a Japanese spirit is different from the amorphous idea of a Japanese national essence associated with wartime mobilization. Instead, as Mori Yoshio has demonstrated, the Taiwanese reading of "Japanese spirit"—*ribunjingshin*—is a decidedly postwar and (post)colonial term. That the Taiwanese usually use the Taiwanese pronunciation *ribunjingshin* rather than the Japanese *nihonseishin* only underscores this colonial difference. Unlike *nihonseishin*, which projects a sense of dedication and commitment to the Japanese nation and the emperor, *ribunjingshin* defines a more quotidian and practical understanding of social etiquette and communal conduct. It is construed less about the nation, and more about everyday lives and their organization. Most Japanese neoconservatives, including Kobayashi Yoshinori, eager to recuperate an imaginary past ideal, often project their own notions of *nihonseishin* onto the Taiwanese *ribunjingshin*. The Taiwanese locution points to attitudes and behaviors that suggest moral and ethical virtues. It points to a wide spectrum of conducts and behaviors that is associated with a greater whole: punctuality, justice, diligence, willingness to abide by the law, responsibility, sincerity, humaneness, and other virtues. It is important to note here that these attitudes are associated not with "Japan" per se, but with the perceived Japanese "period" in contradistinction to the renegade government from the mainland. It is only through the historical trauma of another (post)colonial colonial rule that the Japanese colonial period appears righteous, just, and orderly. Thus the nostalgia for the colonial period—despite its real discrimination and injustice—is projected to underscore the rampant corruption of the "liberation" and the authoritarian regime of the KMT in which former colonial subjects are viewed with suspicion and disdain. By associating *ribunjingshin* with a modern moral and ethical form of conduct for the "greater good," with in fact a philosophy of the public, the formerly colonized also lament its passing in contemporary Japan, where they see rampant social ills that they attribute to an increasingly self-centered populace that has abandoned the notion of the common good. In this critique of contemporary degeneration, the *dōsan* generation shares a similar conservatism with Japanese neoconservatives and sees the regeneration of the Japanese nation as their most urgent calling.

If the nostalgia for *ribunjingshin* is for the period of Japanese rule rather than for Japan itself, the evocation of *ribunjingshin* almost always enforces a contrast with the postliberation rule of the KMT from 1945 to 1987. *Ribunjingshin* then undergirds the imagined period that critiques the (post)colonial era and further emphasizes the schism and incommensurability between "China" and "Taiwan." The contradistinction between Japanese rule and Chinese rule is usually posited as between modernity and primitivity, dignity in defeat and avarice in victory, that overturns the normative relationship between loser and victor in war. The writers uniformly comment on images of the take-over Chinese military as haggard and beggarlike in their appearance and lacking military discipline. Their crassness and idiocy are documented and repeated in several rumors about their inability to understand or use modern technology: a Chinese soldier trying to switch on a light bulb without connecting it to the outlet; another soldier buying a water faucet and being furious at the sales clerk because no water would come out of it after he attached it to a wall. Such repeated stories and caricatures reinforce the conviction that Japan lost to the Americans and not to the Chinese.

The stories of primitive Chinese soldiers reverse the dominant discourse of "retrocession" that justified the KMT rule over Taiwan. In Taiwan, decolonization—unlike in normative Third World discourse—was not about liberation or independence, but about a "retrocession" (*guangfu*) to the fatherland, China; while Third World discourse is about independence, for the Communist Party in China it is about emancipation (*fanshen*) or liberation (*jiefang*). As the KMT maintained its symbolic legitimacy over the representation of China, Chinese "retrocession" of Taiwan meant re-Sinicization of the Taiwanese from their fifty years of "enslavement" (*nuhua*) by the Japanese. It is important to note here the subtle but crucial differences in how Korean and Chinese discourses constructed their internal Other, the collaborators with the Japanese, and the Chinese representation of the Taiwanese subjects. It is instructive that the words for collaborators in Korean and Chinese are "*chinilpa*" (pro-Japanese faction) and "*hanjian*" (traitor to the Han race), respectively, whereas Japanese colonization in Taiwan is apprehended as a period of "enslavement." The Taiwanese are collectively rendered as "slaves" of the Japanese. By describing the colonial period as "enslavement," the KMT not only legitimized itself as a superior culture, but also availed itself of the unconditional power to "un-enslave" its subjects and to expel any remnant of colonial rule in total and by any means necessary. Whereas their internal Other—*chinilpa* and *hanjian*—must be tried, exhibited, and executed, the "slaves," by definition owned by others, are not only "saved" by the nationalists, but also must be "reeducated" and their culture "reconfigured." "Enslavement" therefore led to the need for "eradication" of all traces of colonialism—meaning anything that could be associated with Japanese rule—from language to education, from clothing to architecture. During this time of "transition," Taiwanese intellectuals pleaded for a more moderate process of "translation"—translating what is modern and useful from the Japanese to Chinese. But this was completely ignored in favor of the patriotic process of Sinicization.[11] Taiwanese intellectuals were therefore deprived of any role as active subjects of decolonization. Instead, they became passive objects of re-Sinicization.

The primitivity of the "victorious" army is further compounded by the rampant corruption and brutality of the new regime. All the writers mention the February 28 Incident in 1947. That led to a severe military crackdown in which tens of thousands of Taiwanese were killed and arrested. In this time of turmoil and confusion, the Japanese language was used by the Taiwanese as the only way to distinguish the Taiwanese from the Chinese. A scene from Hou Hsiao-hsien's *Beiqing chengshi* (The city of sadness) brilliantly captures this irony of how the colonial language becomes a means of resisting the "liberating" people." Liberation is followed by the forty-year authoritarian rule of the KMT after they relocated to Taiwan in the wake of their defeat by the Communists. What ensued was a period of white terror aimed at squashing political dissent and exercising ideological control in the name of anti-Communism under the Cold War structure. The KMT launched several anti-Japanese measures to consolidate its rule and to reeducate the Taiwanese from their "slave" mentality. The longing for *ribunjingshin* and the Japanese period, unlike most forms of nostalgia, is not simply a passive and conservative reaction to the status quo or a lamenting of the passing away of a particular privilege. Instead, it is an active demand for reparation and redress. Certainly it should lead to the interrogation of the presumed linear narrative of colonialism → anticolonialism → liberation → nation-building prevalent in most Third Worldist discourse.

Nostalgia for *ribunjingshin* as a counternarrative to Taiwan's second colonization under the nationalist regime thus creates an anti-China attitude in the *dōsan* generation that is both culturalist and racist. Their postliberation experiences consolidated in their minds the notion that the Chinese are prone to lying and therefore untrustworthy, that they always rationalize their actions and are inherently corrupt. From one's own *waishengren* brother-in-law to generalized remarks about rude and shoplifting Chinese tourists, all *waishengren* and mainlanders are conflated and stereotyped, if not demonized, as insidious, corrupt, and haughty. Not only is the Japanese period then rationalized as better and just, but all criticism of Japanese colonialism is hence regarded as Chinese conspiracy and slander. In their resolute anti-China stance, the *dōsan* generation envisions themselves in their twilight years as humble former subjects reminding a degenerating nation of its past grandeur and accomplishments in the midst of China's rise to prominence. The ambiguity and double meaning of *ribunjingshin* and *nihonseishin* thus connect the former colonized's plea for recognition and the former colonizers' desire for national revival. This shared ethos emerges as a mechanism to imagine a future that was denied to the former colonial subjects. They take pains to explain that their opinions about contemporary Japan should not be construed as "criticism" but as "kind advice" from those who were once Japanese. Many lament their old age but hope to awaken and to revitalize Japan through their feeble but genuine acts. They urge the Japanese to develop historical consciousness about Japan's colonial relationship to Taiwan, to rekindle the pride that the

Japanese once had during the colonial period and postwar reconstruction, and to remember the once beautiful, once wonderful nation.

What is clear from this desire for reconnection with Japan and for Japan's revival is the *dōsan* generation's acute sense of threat from a newly powerful China. All the texts present the emergence of China as a danger to the co-prosperity of the region. They still view the new China through the lens of old stereotypes and are unable to reconcile the gap between their "seeing" China's astonishing economic growth and "believing" in their memories of an underdeveloped China. What I would like to suggest is that the anxiety over China and the sense of urgency for reconnection with and revitalization of Japan point to the pronounced shift within the regional order from the modern/colonial model of Japan and/in Asia in which Taiwan was subsumed since the late nineteenth century and throughout the postcolonial postwar years. What this anxiety reveals is precisely the passing of Japan as the sole leader in the region. With the economic and cultural development of South Korea, Taiwan, and the so-called greater China, Japan, for the first time in its modern/colonial history, has to confront its neighbors as equals. This eclipsing of the Japan-centric model is crucial to the neoconservatives' attempt to recuperate the "pride of the Japanese." For the *dōsan* generation, it is also an attempt to make sense of their tumultuous lives under various periods of colonization. It is a desperate yearning for recognition, a truncated identity that with their passing will be forgotten and buried with their remains. Abandoned by Japanese colonialism after Japan's defeat, oppressed by the KMT because of their Japanese heritage, they found no viable channels to express their feelings other than in the privacy of their homes, with their families and friends. That the Japanese neoconservatives became the only group to mobilize their memories and stories is only a testament to the tenacity of the traces of colonialism and the bittersweetness of the postcolonial condition between Japan and Taiwan.

Conclusion

Frantz Fanon said that decolonization is always a violent phenomenon. It is "quite simply the replacing of a certain 'species' of men by another 'species' of men. Without any period of transition, there is a total, complete, and absolute substitution." It is a historical process where "the last shall be first and the first last." This reversal of fortune can take place, he warns us, only "after a murderous and decisive struggle between the two protagonists" (1968: 37). The decolonization process between Japan and Taiwan was violent, but the violence that ensued was not between the colonizer and the colonized, but between the liberating semicolonized and the colonized. Whereas Fanon has cautioned about reproducing the structure of the colonizer under the national bourgeoisie after liberation and the implication of neocolonialism, decolonization in Taiwan produced two different but interrelated trajectories: a process of "recolonization through liberation and decolonization through defeat." Liberation became another form of exerting external control over the natives, inheriting the colonial structure left behind by the former colonizer. In this (post)colonial condition, the last remained last. Japan's defeat meant that the Japanese empire was liquidated without intense struggles in the former colonies: defeat simply replaced decolonization. The first did not become last. It is this paradoxical condition of (post)coloniality that I call the "nondecolonization" between Japan and Taiwan. Nondecolonization, as a historical condition, problematizes the teleological discourse of colonization → decolonization → liberation. My purpose is not to imagine what could have been if there were "true" decolonization. Instead, nondecolonization points to the convoluted and violent process of East Asian (post)coloniality where anti-Japanism and pro-Japanism are only its belated manifestations. Japan has always had an ambivalent relationship to its Asian neighbors. It has viewed itself as simultaneously part of Asia and apart from Asia—racially similar but culturally superior. This modern/colonial perspective is fast becoming outdated, given the rise of China and other Asian nations such as South Korea and Taiwan. It is telling that recently the resident Korean critic Kang Sanjun has asked if Japan is willing to be "the orphan of Asia" if it continues to serve as a client state of the United States and ignore its Asian neighbors. It is ironic that Kang uses the word "orphan" to describe Japan today. *Orphan of Asia*, a book written in Japanese by the Taiwanese author Wu Zhouliu during the war years, describes the protagonist's painful realization of a Taiwanese identity after being rejected by both Japanese colonialism and Chinese nationalism.[12] For the *dōsan* generation, the desire for recognition derives from the ambivalence of their colonial and (post) colonial identities. Ke Desan writes that when he visited Japan during colonial times he was asked by the Japanese where he came from. After he told them Taiwan, he was asked if he were related to the headhunting aborigines. In (post)colonial times, the questions are still where you are from, and why you speak Japanese so fluently. Postwar and (post)colonial Japanese simply cannot fathom the existence of people who once were Japanese. This inability to relate to the former colonial subject is symptomatic of the larger forgetting of colonialism in postwar Japan. For the *dōsan* generation, unfortunately, time may not be on their side.

FIVE. "In the Name of Love":
Critical Regionalism and Co-Viviality in Post–East Asia

Love is the only force capable of transforming an enemy to a friend.
—MARTIN LUTHER KING JR.

Let me begin with two images. During the fall 2012 anti-Japanese rallies in China—as with the 2005 protests but arguably with more intensity and regularity—images, videos, tweets, and chats inspired by these rallies proliferated on social media such as Sina Weibo, the most popular microblog site in China. Because many Japanese-branded stores were vandalized by the protesters, store owners and consumers went to great lengths to demonstrate their patriotism (or more likely to deflect their peers' patriotism) such as darkening and taping over Japanese brand names on their electronics or insisting on the stores' Chinese ownership. The first photo shows the storefront advertising Japanese brands Nikon and Sony in an unspecified Chinese city.

In the photo, just below the yellow Nikon sign, is a row of smaller but brightly lit red neon lights displaying the following phrases: "Down with Little Japs; Nab Aoi [last name] Sola Alive; Return Diaoyu Islands to Us!" There is no doubt that this electronic sign was meant to shelter the store from angry demonstrators, as "little Japs" and "the Diaoyu Islands" clearly express solidarity with Chinese nationalist sentiments. What then, do we make of the reference to the famed former Japanese adult video star Aoi Sola? Japanese adult videos have dominated the Asian (black) market with Aoi as one of its biggest former stars. As she gradually moved to mainstream acting, Aoi made her debuts in other Asian entertainment markets. In March 2008, she appeared in a Thai film, *Hormones*, playing the role of a Japanese tourist. In May 2009, she appeared in the Korean TV drama *The Korean Classroom*. In April 2011, she starred in the Indonesian horror film *Suster Keramas 2*. However, by 2014 it was China where she had the most fans, including among them women who do not consume adult videos. In China at that time Aoi had more than thirteen million followers on Sina Weibo and was affectively referred to as "Teacher Cang" by her adoring admirers.[1]

On September 14, amid the anti-Japanese protests, she posted on her Sina Weibo account some fetching calligraphy calling for Sino-Japanese "friendship." Aoi's seemingly innocent, if not naive, plea for peace predictably met with mixed reactions, from mockery to admiration, from scorn to tacit approval. While many of Aoi's presumably male sympathizers urged her not to get into politics (a messy men's business, they say), most responses were either crudely sexualized references to her previous profession or were light teasing with sexual innuendos. What we see here in Aoi's "public" calling for "friendship" between the two nations and the "private" experience of her Chinese fans denouncing her is an incommensurability of "love" for her with "love" for the country. Those fans who insisted that Aoi should stay out of politics substituted one type of intimacy (self-pleasure, visual delight) for another (love of the nation, love of the race). By "capturing her alive," as the slogan appears in the photo, it at least temporarily resolves the contradiction between public and pubic (?) desires, satisfying the love for the country and taking possession of their "idol." What we have here then, whether coarse or soft sexism, is a masculinist discourse that repeats the old idiom of "violate the enemy's women": one that expresses the love for the nation as a public performance of patriotism, the other one that represses love for a porn star, or rather for her performance that is presumably practiced in private. What links these seemingly incommensurable affects is carnality and masculinity. Perhaps instead of love, we should characterize the second affect as lust. Unlike love, lust, as an appetite, is believed to be indiscriminate as well as indifferent to its object's subjective states and wishes, whereas love signifies reciprocity feeling and exclusivity.

The second image circulated widely on the internet appears to express the opposite sentiment to the previous one. It shows a young Chinese woman, eyes cast down, holding a poster that reads "We've overcome war, earthquake and flood. This is not fascism; our territory is never based on fighting, smashing or burning. This is not the Cultural Revolution. The whole world watched our Olympics. Please stop the violence. I remember, our country is filled with LOVE." Contrary to the masculinist, sexualized, and vindictive nationalist sign, this simple declaration, written in black characters on white paper, is much more moderate and critical of the mob mentality of the anti-Japanese protesters. If we can borrow Frantz Fanon's formulation of racism and call the first "vulgar nationalism," we might characterize the second as a form of "polite nationalism." Differentiating this from fascism and the Cultural Revolution—evils of the past—stressing the resiliency of the Chinese people over man-made and natural disasters, and drawing on the success of the recent Beijing Olympics as a sign of progress and development, the poster urges the protesters to stop the violence. What made this claim of benign nationalism possible is "ai," or love, written in an enlarged character. As with Aoi's call for "friendship," a banal if not empty gesture of diplomatic naivete, the appeal to love as a unifying principle for the Chinese nation is not without its own problems. As Michael Hardt (2011) has argued, this type of love is identitarian and nontransformative. It is love of the same that characterizes nationalism, fascism, and racism alike, although to different degrees and intensities. For Hardt, a properly political concept of love must resist a unifying impulse and embrace differences and multiplicity. It must be love of the stranger and open to the power to create new social bonds and affiliations. What political concept of love can we imagine that will transcend both vulgar and polite nationalism? What can love, as a political concept, do to create new affinities and subjectivities that enable us to imagine relationships in East Asia beyond fundamentalist political conflicts and liberal cultural exchanges? In this chapter, I examine four representations of love—or representations of the political concept of love—in postwar postcolonial East Asia that offer glimpses of possibility for transnational and subnational intimacies.[2]

I examine the instantiations of love in four texts: *Gojira* (1954), *Death by Hanging* (1968), *Mohist Attack* (1992–1996), and *My Own Breathing* (1999). The choice of these texts is not arbitrary. Some have already been discussed in previous chapters, hence affording these texts the possibilities of multiple and differentiated readings. I suggest that they represent four possible political concepts of love that allow us to glimpse the possibilities of affective belonging that transcend love of the nation and love of the same. Their specific historicities suggest variable possibilities and impossibilities conditioned and delimited by their respective political contexts. I preliminarily configure them as "postwar," "postcolonial," "post-bubble," and "post-nation," respectively. By focusing on the love triangle in *Gojira*, I demonstrate the transition from "traditional" to "modern" love in postwar Japan. However, instead of privileging the modern over the traditional, I argue that the realization and materialization of the modern form of coupling depends on sacrificing the "traditional" form of nonromantic engagement. In this regard, a "traditional" arrangement of marriage is not outside modern, romantic love, but is its very condition of possibility. In *Death by Hanging*, we see the refusal of R, the postcolonial subject, to identify with the Korean nation through his love for "Sister." Despite his affection for "Sister," who represents the conscience of anticolonial nationalism, R continues to struggle with his diasporic condition as a Korean living in Japan, and he finds the unification with the Korean nation not commensurable with his present plight. Reinscribing the notion of an impartial love of Mohism, *Mohist Attack*, a serial manga, critiques the history of warfare that links impartial love with antiwarism. This impartial love rearticulates a linkage between Japan and China as having a common ancestry amid the growing nationalist chauvinism in post-bubble Japan. Lastly, *My Own Breathing* redeems the shame of the "comfort women" through the unconditional love between mother and daughter amidst the continuous deferral and denial of apologies and compensations by the patriarchal Korean and Japanese nation-states. It is not in the official public realm of diplomacy, but in private intimacy that the politics of reconciliation become possible. The analyses are not simply different instantiations of intimacy, but glimpses of relationality outside of heteronormative and state-sanctioned politics of reconciliation. In short, they allow us to imagine love, otherwise.

Gojira, Romantic Love, and Postwar Japan

As Japan's "first postwar media event," *Gojira* (1954) was a landmark in Japanese filmmaking (Kushner 2006: 41). It not only marked Japan's return to the international stage, but it also was the first film not to have to undergo American Occupation censorship; it was the first film to generate a franchise, and it engendered an adaptation (a very bad one nonetheless) to Hollywood's monster-flick genre. Susan Napier has argued that *Gojira* operates on a number of ideological registers (1993: 331–32). First, it demonizes American nuclear science in an obvious reference to the atomic tragedies of Hiroshima and Nagasaki. (Incidentally, thirty minutes of references to the two sites of nuclear devastation were deleted from the American version.) Second, the film ends with the triumph of "good" Japanese science against the evil and menacing monster— via a dramatic ending in which the Japanese scientist, Serizawa, using his oxygen destroyer, vanquishes the nuclear beast—thus signifying a "rewriting of history" wherein Japan, and not the United States, emerges as the world's savior. Serizawa's sacrificial humanism, as opposed to wartime fascist militarism, conjures a new Japan that is antinuclear and symbolically "anti-American," and, at least temporarily, reverses the power dynamics between the two countries. What is, however, less frequently observed by critics of the film is the love triangle between Serizawa, Emiko (Professor Yamane's daughter), and Ogata, the salvage-ship captain. Serizawa, a colleague of Yamane's, has an arranged marriage to Emiko. But Emiko is attracted to Ogata and decides to break off the engagement. Serizawa, perhaps still interested in Emiko, shows and demonstrates to her his secret experiment and invention, the lethal oxygen destroyer, and warns her not to tell anyone about it. Shocked by the power of this secret weapon and eager to defeat the menacing monster, Emiko, ignoring Serizawa's warning, tells Ogata about the weapon and they try to convince Serizawa to unleash it on Gojira. Despite much prodding and agonizing, Serizawa initially rejects their plea, citing the danger of the oxygen destroyer falling into the wrong hands. However, witnessing Gojira's devastation and the agony of the injured, and after listening to songs by schoolgirls broadcast on television, Serizawa changes his mind. What is germane here is that Serizawa's sacrifice not only destroys Gojira (and Serizawa himself), but also allows Ogata and Emiko, the symbol of postwar individualism, democracy, and romantic love, to prevail. Serizawa's sacrificial love (for humanity and for Emiko) thus resolves two crises, national and personal.

Anthony Giddens (1992) has argued that "romantic love," based on already-established gender norms (hence unequal) and sexuality, has given way to "confluent love," which is based less on complementarity between the sexes than on contingency and lifestyle choices led by feminine emancipation and autonomy, developments that have the potential of democratizing sexuality and leading to personal freedom. Giddens is talking about sexuality and democratization in late-industrial societies such as the United States. However, his distinction between "romantic love" and "confluent love" is useful in thinking about the historicity of love within modernity and its increased democratization.[3] Pushing further back in history and focusing on three case studies, William Reddy (2012) argues that "romantic love" emerged in twelfth-century Europe as a way of coping, if not deflecting, the theological chastisement regarding desire-as-appetite. The dichotomy between "true love" and "desire-as-appetite" undergirded the Western notion of "romantic love." Analyzing the South Asian and Japanese contexts in similar historical periods, Reddy found that the binarism between love and desire did not exist in the European counterparts. Both Giddens and Reddy alert us to the conservatism of "romantic love," despite its seemingly modern, individualistic, and progressive guises. For *Gojira*, we need to apprehend the tension between "romantic love" and "arranged marriage" and their resolution in the context of postwar Japan and the symbolic anti-Americanism discussed in chapter 1. While Serizawa invents and possesses new technology to destroy Gojira, he himself is a victim and relic of a recent past. We learn that his blinded eye is an injury sustained during the Pacific war; his respect for Dr. Yamane and his desire to consummate the arranged marriage with Emiko represent the hierarchical structure of interpersonal relations that the supposedly liberated and democratizing postwar Japan has tried to eradicate with the assistance of the American Occupation.

The injured and disfigured Serizawa, much like the radiation-infected Gojira, is a figure representing the trauma of war and nuclear devastation. It is therefore not surprising that both Serizawa and Gojira have to perish (or be repressed in history) so a new Japan can be born. However, the film is far from a straightforward endorsement of postwar values such as democracy, demilitarization, and freedom. As a man of devotion and duty (characteristics that supposedly contributed to fascism), yet much like the monster itself, Serizawa evokes feelings of lament, nostalgia, and gallantry from the audience. In this regard, compared to Serizawa's sacrifice, the romantic love between Emiko and Ogata can only appear selfish and cowardly. In a subtle overturning of the postwar value system, the ghosts of war and nuclear devastation return to haunt the new Japan. Serizawa sacrifices for humanity and modern love. Put differently, Serizawa's love extends beyond individuals, or the Japanese, to humankind. Modern love, symbolized by the coupling and unification of Emiko and Ogata, is made possible only with the demise of a "traditional" marital arrangement. In this sense, a truly postwar modern Japan is conditioned on the passing of "premodern" practices, such as arranged marriage, and yet that "traditional love" is expansive and redemptive. Here *Gojira* questions the facile transition of Japan from wartime militarism to postwar democracy. While it depicts the romantic conjoining of Emiko and Ogata, the film's denouement requires a different form of love to actualize itself.

Death by Hanging, Love, Nation, and Postcolonial Japan

Death by Hanging (1968) is arguably one of Oshima Nagisa's most daring and critically acclaimed films in the wake of the failure of anti-Anpo protests.[4] If *Gojira* signifies a transition from postwar to the end of the postwar era—from a defeated country to a revitalized economy, thanks to America's "reverse course"—*Death by Hanging* highlights the shift from political defeat to cultural avant-gardism. Influenced by Brechtian aesthetics, the film uses the debate over the death penalty as a prelude to exposing the discrimination faced by the resident Koreans and the colonial history that brought them to Japan in the first place. With black humor and stinging criticism, *Death by Hanging* is a composite of comedy, tragedy, and political satire. What I want to focus on here, however, is the relationship between R, the protagonist, and the woman that R calls his "sister" in one of the seven intertitles in the film. Based on the actual correspondence between the murderer in the 1958 incident, a resident Korean journalist, and their relationship, "sister" becomes the means by which R will accept external confirmation of his Korean identity as a first step toward effectively *becoming* R.[5] What I want to suggest in this sequence is both the personification of Korean nationalism through "sister," and R's ambivalence toward that politics of unification—between South and North Koreas, R and sister—despite his "love" for sister. In short, while in love with sister, R, as a resident Korean, rejects the double blackmail of Japanese assimilationism and Korean nationalism. As the Japanese officials struggle to have R recognize himself as R, the murdered girl transmorphs and appears as "sister" in front of R.[6] R asks the sister whether he is the R that she knows, and she responds by saying, "Yes, you are a Korean called R," affirming R's Korean ancestry and current identity. Sister further reminds R that he began to use R instead of his Japanese name when he was "awakened to Korean nationalism" (*minzoku ishiki*). Furthermore, sister introduces the oppression of Korean women historically. She tells R as he touches her skin: "R, you're touching the Korean skin that bears the long, painful history of the Korean race. When the race is sad, we women are especially sad. There are no women of my age from the southern part of Korea who do not bear scars. They are beaten by their fathers, injured by their husbands, and some of them have committed suicide, slitting their wrists." One Japanese official then interjects a narrative of the long history of oppression on the Korean Peninsula and the thirty-six years of Japanese colonial rule. Sister then reminds R that at the night school he was "a young Korean among Japanese who knew his Korean race" (*rippana chōsenjin*). She then implores him to atone for his crime by striving for unification and the prosperity of his country. The exchanges between sister and the Japanese officials further incriminate Japan and the colonial past that forcibly brought Koreans to Japan. As sister puts it succinctly: "R's crime was caused by Japanese imperialism and thus Japan has no right whatsoever to punish him."

Finally, sister asks R, "We're going to work for the unity of our country, will you follow me?" R, however, remains silent. "Why don't you answer?" she asks. After a pause, R answers, "Maybe I don't remember very well. Being a revolutionary doesn't seem to fit R though I am trying to be and think like him." "You mean you don't care about the unification of your country?" sister interrogates. To that nationalist demand, R replies, "it doesn't quite fit" (*pittari shinaidesu*). To that, sister can only retort: "When did you change? R, you're no longer R. You're no longer a Korean! You've lost R's spirit and you've lost the Korean spirit. You're simply a culprit, a murderer!" R's nonrecognition of himself as a revolutionary Korean destroys the fantasy of nationalism. For sister, R's crime was a Korean crime. More important, R's crime "is the only way for a Korean to wreak revenge upon the Japanese. In the name of the Japanese nation, the Japanese have murdered innumerable Koreans. However, we who belong nowhere (without nation) can only take personal revenge on the Japanese. The world is upside down [*yuganda*]." The pride and sorrow of the Koreans, sister continues, are subsumed into this murder. Against this identification between the national and the personal, while ignoring the diasporic and the postcolonial, R's response is not what she expected: "Sister, if what you described is really the way R is . . . then I am not R at all." What is important for the context of our discussion is R's ambivalence about various forms of identification, or unification—between the personal and the national, between the two Koreas, and between himself and sister. What the film does here is, while allowing the critique of Japanese colonialism and

Korean patriarchy to present themselves through sister's enunciations, it disallows a facile reduction of the resident Korean as representative of anti-Japan Korea and its colonial wound. The otherness of a resident Korean, precisely because of the resident's always-already colonized and diasporic status, "just doesn't quite fit" the discourse of nationalism, even if it is an anti-imperialist nationalism. Through this reading, the love for sister is not reduced to, or made equivalent to, love of the nation. This ambivalence or hesitation, while allowing personal love for another human being, does not collapse it into love of the nation, as is prevalent in Third World nationalist discourse.

Mohist Attack, Impartial Love, and Post-Bubble Japan

Mohist Attack (*Bokkō*), a historic novella by Sakemi Ken'ichi (1991), was serialized as a manga by Mori Hideki from 1992 to 1996 in Big Comics.[7] Set in the Warring States Period of 370 BC China, the manga depicts Kakuri, the lone adherent of the Mohist philosophy of "impartial love" (*kenai* in Japanese, *jian ai* in Chinese readings) and "nonaggression" (*hikō*; *fei gong*), and his attempts at defending weaker states from stronger ones by using various tactics of fortification. The plot is complicated by the fact that Kakuri not only has to defend the city-state from attackers, but also has to fend off assassins who are his former comrades at the Mohist school, thus creating a subplot that accentuates Kakuri's battle skills, his commitment to the Mohist thoughts and practice, and also his precarious situation. The once venerable Mohist school has degenerated, moving further away from the teachings of impartial love and the condemnation of aggressive war, and has availed itself to the powerful Qin state by offering itself as a mercenary service to attack others. Banished from the Mohist school for his refusal to ignore the request to defend the weaker states, Kakuri sets out on a treacherous journey. What needs to be defended is therefore not only the weak states, but Mohist philosophy itself.

Pertinent to our discussion is the manga's ironic ending that criticizes Japan's history of warmongering. The story has Kakuri being forced to leave the Chinese proper after one of his patron kings decides to release him of his service with a small group of adults and children. It becomes clear that where Kakuri and his entourage have ended up is none other than the land of the rising sun. This episode clearly references the myth of Japanese ancestry as originating in mainland China under the rule of the First Emperor. The myth has Chinese men and women dispatched by the emperor in search of an elixir of life. It is said that they ended up in Japan and became the progenitors of present-day Japanese people. The manga ends by fast-forwarding to the present where Kakuri returns to Japan as a terra-cotta warrior on display in a department store. The caption reads: "What would Kakuri think about the history of Japan?" following a series of images depicting Japan's military aggressions, both internal and external, throughout its history. The critique here is that Japan, despite its origins in the teachings of impartial love and anti-aggression embodied by Kakuri and his followers, has continuously waged wars against its own people and others. Unlike postwar pacifism that eschewed the difficult question of Japanese colonialism and imperialism, *Mohist Attack* not only reconstructs a mythological connectivity with imperial China, but also lays bare the various acts of war waged throughout Japan's history.

Impartial love and antiwar are intrinsically related. To love the other is to exclude the possibilities of aggression (or partiality) toward the other. "When states and cities do not attack and make war on one another, and families and individuals do not overthrow or injure one another, is it a harm to the world or a benefit? Surely it is a benefit!" This benefit comes from "loving others and trying to benefit them," and when people do so, they are motivated by universality and not partiality (Watson 2003: 42). This "universalism" is an attack on the Confucian notion of "partial love," in which people differentiate their treatment of others in a carefully scaled manner depending on familial relationships and other factors, such as friendship, political roles, relative need, and broad social implications.

As a manga genre, *Mohist Attack*'s critical anti-aggression and impartial love stand in direct contrast with subsequent manga in the 2000s that advocate nationalism and racism against other Asians. These manga draw radical differences and illustrate the incommensurability between Japan and other Asian nations, usually China and Korea, and promote the sentiment of hate. Depicting the Chinese as self-centered, irrational, and abnormal, *Manga Chūgoku nyūmon* (A manga intro to China) (2005) by Jōji Akiyama presents a history of modern China mired in continuous crisis and turmoil. Recent anti-Japan movements in China are seen as the redirection of internal anxiety and discontent among the Chinese people and have escalated to "hating" Japan (54). Akiyama's manga depicts the Chinese as cannibalistic, militaristic, and expansionist. Under the Chinese threat, the manga exposes the social ills caused by China's economic "success" and urges Japan to re-militarize in order to confront the rise of China. In a similarly bifurcating construction of self and other, while also demonizing the other, the best-selling *Kenkanryū* (Hating the Korean wave) (2005) by Yamano Sharin makes South Korea its target of derision. Paying scant attention to the popularity of contemporary Korean culture in Japan, as implied in the title, the manga intends to expose the "true" history of Japan-Korean relations. Its premise is that everything taught about Korea in Japan has been wrong, including the history of the colonial period and the discrimination against "resident Koreans" in Japan. Cleverly deploying the narrative of self-discovery through informal knowledge production, the manga has its male protagonist awaken to the "truth" of Korea through various staged debates and self-study. Both the Yamano and Akiyama works were published in the mid-2000s. Their fanning of nationalist sentiments only point to the shifting geopolitical position in East Asia where Japan's once dominant status is no longer assured with the rise of China and popularity of the Korean Wave. The rearticulation of a shared past/ancestry and the revoking of a third philosophical tradition other than Confucianism and Daoism, the "impartial love" and "nonaggression" praxis of Mohism not only critiques all warfare, including Japan's, but also advocates a commonality that rejects the ideology of national competition in the era of neoliberal globalization.

My Own Breathing, Unconditional Love, and the Politics of Reconciliation

The fourth example of the political concept of love attempts a reconciliation, not on a national level but between family members in healing the "colonial wound." I argue that in the wake of continuing denial and neglect by the Japanese government (with complicity from the South Korean state), the space of domestic intimacy subverts the public discussion of national reconciliation that insists on state-to-state negotiations, apologies, and compensations.[8]

One of the main characters in Byung Young-Joo's *My Own Breathing* is Kim Yun Shim, a former comfort woman who received the Jeon Tae Il Award for her realistic portrayal of life in the Military Sexual Slavery Unit. Kim recounts her tumultuous and unhappy life after "liberation": betrothed at sixteen by her mother, divorced by her husband due to her barrenness, and remarried at the age of twenty-six. However, her daughter has cerebral palsy and is mute, most likely because of Kim's physical illness sustained while in the Military Sexual Slavery Unit. Kim ran away with her baby because she was afraid her past would be revealed. In "those days when a woman had syphilis, she wasn't a human." In one of the most poignant scenes of the film, the director interviews Kim and her daughter, Sun Ye Sook. The mother and daughter sit next to each other, a measured distance apart, with Kim closer to her sewing machine that she uses for her job as a tailor. Byung asks Kim how much she thinks her daughter knows about her experience. "She doesn't know much," Kim answers and smiles confidently while her daughter sits knowingly next to her. From the daughter's facial expression, it becomes apparent that she knows more than what her mother thinks she does. After several more exchanges with the director, Kim assures her that her daughter does not know and definitely has not read her award-winning book.

Kim then uses sign language and asks her daughter, "Do you know about my book?" as she looks at her daughter to confirm that she does not. Much to Kim's surprise, the daughter, using sign language, responds, "I know. I read it. Yes, while you were in America." As Sun responds to Byung's queries about the content of the book, Kim looks on with anguish and concern while continuing to tell the director, "She probably doesn't know." When the director asks, "You know? You know everything?," the daughter nods. As the camera zooms in on Kim's surprised look, the director reiterates what the daughter has told her about how she knows why her mother was kidnapped. "So she read the book, that book?" Kim queries, still in disbelief. "Yes, I think she did," Byung confirms. "Wow, she did read the book," Kim says, while continuing to look away and pretending to work on her sewing machine. As if unable to suppress her surprise and seeking consolation, Kim suddenly turns to her daughter and asks if her grandchild has read the book and tells her that she should not have. Kim once again turns away, and we see Sun smile with a sense of satisfaction while nodding and glancing at her mother. Kim again turns to her daughter, but this time she taps at Sun's back and smiles. The daughter smiles back. Sun then uses sign language to express her gratitude to her mother: "She worried a lot about me. Two years ago she began coming to see me often. She thinks about me a lot. She doesn't like it that I am just getting by. She wanted me to be happy just the way we used to be. She comes here and helps me a lot." The scene then ends with the following text from Kim: "The past which I will never forget in my life. My daughter who can't speak forever because of this unfortunate mother. My daughter who I love to death. My tragedy shouldn't continue on to her life. The brutal and merciless Japanese soldiers. I hope there will be no more war. The past I will never forget in my life. I must keep it to myself forever. "

A shameful secret that the mother has kept away from her daughter. A tragedy that the mother would not want to wish upon the daughter. The gratitude the daughter has for the caring mother. An acknowledgment of mutual love and struggle that overcomes the memory of the atrocity inflicted on both mother and daughter and that transcends shame. The demand for justice has enabled these old women to come forward and testify. In doing so, they overcome the patriarchal nationalist shame imposed on them. The scene portrays the undying and unconditional love between mother and daughter who are bound by violence and pain, and the acknowledgment of this truth overcomes the mother's shame.

Conclusion

It is important to underscore that the four political concepts of love I discuss here are not transcendental or universal categories, although they might appear to be so as any enunciation of love tends to be. Instead, they are historically specific sentiments and emotions borne out of political necessity where resolutions and reconciliations are not yet available or possible.

In *Political Emotions: Why Love Matters for Justice* (2013), the philosopher/legal scholar Martha Nussbaum proposes that to sustain stability and motivation in a liberal society, the cultivation of public emotions is essential to inducing strong commitments to justice in citizens. Appropriate sentiments such as sympathy and love, she argues, are necessary to guard against division and hierarchy. Nussbaum's intervention is an important one, especially as a philosopher and proponent of liberalism, because historically liberal thinkers have not resolved the fundamental problem: How can a "decent" society do more for stability and motivation in cultivating public emotions without becoming illiberal and dictatorial? Nussbaum's book is provocative and touches on crucial issues that this book has tried to address, albeit from a postcolonial perspective. However, I want to take up two of Nussbaum's arguments and use them to extend some of my own theses in this chapter and throughout the book. I want in particular to address the problem of the nation as the unit of analysis and political emotions as eudaimonistic.

Because Nussbaum's central concern is liberalism and society, her unit of analysis understandably is the nation. Following the works of Giuseppe Mazzinni and other nineteenth-century nationalists, Nussbaum sees the nation as a necessary "fulcrum" for leveraging global concern by extending generous sentiments to all humanity.[9] The nation also provides Nussbaum with a good "historical particularity" for the formation of political emotions (17). In this regard, she also defends patriotic sentiments, suggesting that internationalists such as Comte, Mill, and Tagore all provided the nation with an "honored place" in their account of "extended sympathy" (207). She writes: "In loving the nation, people can, if all goes well, embrace general political principles—but in a motivationally efficacious way. The public love we need, then, includes love of the nation, and a love that conceives of the nation not just a set of abstract principles, but as a particular entity, with a specific history, specific physical features, and specific aspirations that inspire devotion" (207). Nussbaum then uses speeches of historical figures in the United States and India (George Washington, Abraham Lincoln, Martin Luther King Jr., Mohandas Gandhi, and Jawaharlal Nehru) to demonstrate how their respective articulations of patriotism can be taught successfully in schools and provide an aspiring nation strength in its struggle for justice.

While not denying the continued relevance of the nation as a unit of analysis, Nussbaum's resort to nineteenth- and twentieth-century theories and figures to justify a "good" patriotism that has the potential to extend and transform these patriotic sentiments into a liberal internationalism seems anachronistic, given the rapidly changing configuration of economic globalization, new social media technology, and transnational mass culture that are simultaneously breaking down and building up nationalist sentiments. Furthermore, the examples she gives are all situated in anticolonial, nation-building processes that look at the nation as the locus of deliverance and emancipation. Yet under today's neoliberalist global capitalism, the role of the nation seems to have become more of an enabler for capital flows and profit making than for providing the kind of aspiration toward justice and equality that Nussbaum attributes to patriotic sentiments. The increased "clash of nationalisms" in East Asia, with anti-Japanism as one of its symptoms, only underscores the tenacity of nationalism's hold on the people, especially those facing increasingly precarious livelihoods under the very capitalist development that nation-states are implementing.

Nussbaum's normative philosophy of public emotions and favorable patriotism as capable of producing "extended sympathy" to others beyond a particular nation seems to correspond to the neo-nationalism of Katō Norihiro that we observed in chapter 1, a neo-nationalism that ultimately provides an alibi for the nation-state indefinitely to defer its responsibility for Japan's colonial rule and its war victims. Katō has argued that for Japan to take responsibility for its Asian victims, it must first constitute a "community of repentance" for its two million Japanese war dead. This rather convoluted logic, while addressing an inherent contradiction of postwar Japan by relegating questions of empire secondary to nation reconstitution, continues to marginalize the horrid experience of others in its fallen empire, as well as the Japanese traumatized by Japanese colonial violence themselves. I do not mean to suggest that the nation, or, more precisely, the nation-state, is irrelevant in today's project of political reconciliation. Given that the empire was claimed and wars were waged in the name of the nation and the emperor, and that governments are currently the only recognized entities of bilateral diplomacy between countries, the role of the nation remains important for victims' demands for reparation and recognition. Furthermore, as Karatani Kōjin (2014) has argued, capital, nation, and state constitute a Borromean knot that modulates, corroborates, and reinforces each other, even in the time of globalization where the nation and the state are supposedly weakened if not irrelevant under the transnationalization of capital.

Nevertheless, the nation form poses notable difficulties for those in the former imperialist state who have opposed their nation's violent history. How would they negotiate their involvements and "implications" as subjects of the imperialist nation and its dissenters? Where some might completely disidentify with the nation-state (as in the case of the feminist scholar Ueno Chizuko) or prioritize one's identification with the nation (as with Katō), is there another option? In "Decolonialization and Assumption of War Responsibility" (2000), the Japanese critic Hanasaki Kōhei argues that in light of the Japanese state's evasion of responsibility for the war and for the incomplete decolonization process within its former empire, a "provisional" identification with the Japanese state and nation is necessary. He writes:

In the face of the accusation that the Japanese as a whole are an accessory to this cover-up, I take the stand that as long as I was born as a member of the colonizer nation state, and am still positioned in a historical situation where the decolonialization of Japan is not complete, I would provisionally take upon myself the definition of being a "Japanese," the definition that is given to me by other people and that puts me into the national Japanese collective. I say "provisionally" because I do not think I should remain forever passively defined and bound by this given relationality. Japanese colonial rule as viewed from the colonized peoples presents itself as nothing other than national oppression by the Japanese as a race. The colonized peoples thus take the Japanese race to task for their colonial responsibility. In the context of decolonialization, this identification of the nation state with the race is grounded in both imagery and reality. (78)

Hanasaki is careful not to collapse responsibility as equally shared by all people who belong to a nation-state as that gesture itself would be nationalistic. (The primary example of this nationalistic rhetoric that made war responsibility ambiguous is Prime Minister Higashikuninomiya's doctrine of "national confession of Japanese war guilt.") Instead, Hanasaki's "provisional" identification should be apprehended as a disposition, an acknowledgment of what Tessa Morris-Suzuki has termed historical "implication" (2005: 25). It is not an acceptance of guilt on behalf of the nation-state, but rather a "strategic essentialism" that opens oneself up toward the Other for a possible dialogical relationship. Without this initial vulnerability, a sense of one's implication within historical forces not of one's choosing, there will be no reconciliation. The ultimate goal for co-viviality is to transcend the nation-state system toward a transborder collaboration.

For Hanasaki, this disposition is an individual choice and free will. It is a provisional identity one has to become. It also points to the paradox of Japanese postcoloniality where flexible subjectivity in postcolonial discourse is incompatible with a rather rigid body (the Japanese state) that still has yet to assume colonial and wartime responsibilities. Creating this postcolonial relationship is, however, the task of not only the former colonizer (or the entity conditionally identified as the former colonizer), but also the formerly colonized, or those who identified with the formerly colonized. Given the violence of colonialism, the desire for a collective identity that arose from resistance to colonial assimilation is understandable. However, this "traditionalism" (*dentōshugi*), or the insistence on protecting this tradition for the sake of tradition, Hanasaki Kōhei argues, amounts to a nonproductive conservatism that ultimately undermines the creativity and energy of development from generation to generation (2001: 120). By provisionally identifying with the nation and assuming responsibilities not of one's own, Hanasaki's decolonialization interrogates and criticizes the role of the nation without privileging it as a step toward political reconciliation and co-viviality.

The four texts I have analyzed, albeit through a very selective reading of love, are intended to historicize "modern" love and posit the possibilities of love as a political concept. In *Gojira*, I identified the interdependent relationship between "traditional" and "modern" love; in *Death by Hanging*, I argued that the liminal status of the resident Korean obliges R to reject unification while allowing personal love to persist; in *Mohist Attack*, an implicit "impartial love" constitutes a self-reflexive critique of war through the concept of "anti-aggression as an alternative to conservative pacifism," and, finally, in *My Own Breathing*, I suggest the intimacy of unconditional love as a way to rethink reconciliation outside the national frame. What fundamentally motivates love is one's relationship to others and how love can exist in various forms without being reduced to coupling, unification, and sameness. Furthermore, precisely because of Japan's legacies of empire, military aggression, nuclear disaster, and environmental degradation, rethinking the history of Japanese radicalism can potentially offer alternatives to the current political stalemates in East Asia. Finding alternatives, I believe, is crucial as the region is increasingly facing similar struggles and crises from the sense of precariousness and social anxiety due to the growing liberalization of economies under global capitalism and from environmental degeneration due to an unfettered developmentalism perpetrated under the guise of nationalism. To this end, the political concept of love must be apprehended in the context of common crises and collaborative work. East Asian nations must strive to overcome growing nationalist sentiments and, in their place, to create aspirations that are antiwar and antimilitaristic and that respect the suffering all their peoples have endured, and this must happen not only for the sake of the past, but also for the future—not just for the dead, but for the yet to come. A politics of reconciliation outside of the nation-state mandate and the struggle for future generations are explored in the next chapter.

six. Reconciliation Otherwise:
Intimacy, Indigeneity, and the Taiwan Difference

There have been important scholarly interventions to make Taiwan legible in the international context: remapping its particular position in the capitalist world system (Jameson 1995), citing its ambivalent and ironic (in) significance in globalization (Shih 2003), and critiquing its southward subimperialist ambitions (Chen 2000). These provocations and theorization notwithstanding, interests in Taiwan or Taiwan studies remain marginal in Euro-American academia, especially compared to the preoccupation with the so-called rise of China. The aim of this chapter is not to overturn the historical and political subordination of Taiwan as an object of study. The facile reversal of Taiwan's "minor" to that of a "major" (or hegemonic) status, hence justifying our analytical attention and intellectual investment, would risk reproducing the power dynamics and the desire of a capital nation-state (Karatani 2014) that the aforementioned critical writings on Taiwan have tried to undo. It is therefore from what Masao Miyoshi (1991) has called an "off center"—a liminal but not invisible—position of critique that I inquire the cultural and political possibility of Taiwan in its marginalization. I do so by attending to two "particularities" of Taiwan in East Asia: the presence of indigenous populations and the supposed intimacy with its former Japanese colonizers.

The original inhabitants, or *yuanzumin* as they are officially called today, comprised approximately 2 percent (500,000) of the total population of Taiwan, which is similar to the ratio of indigenous peoples in Canada and Australia. Encountering and enduring multiple colonial rules like other indigenous peoples in the world, the indigenous people of Taiwan suffered similar cases of extermination, forced relocation, economic dispossession, and cultural annihilation. It is only recently that social movements demanding political rights, economic justice, and cultural autonomy have gained traction in Taiwan's public sphere. As figures of minoritarianism and underdevelopment under colonial and postcolonial regimes, the yuanzumin have been accordingly denigrated and/or romanticized, depending on dominant political exigencies and instrumentalism. Unlike the anti-Japanese sentiments that people readily displayed in China and South Korea, it is often observed that people in Taiwan, especially the so-called *benshengren*, or Taiwanese people, are pro-Japanese. Whereas China and South Korea unequivocally denounce the ills of Japanese imperialism and colonization, Taiwan seems to laud the benefits of colonial modernity. Analyzing these Taiwan differences, I am interested in how indigeneity and intimacy offer the potential to rethink questions of reconciliation outside of the state-centric model of political negotiation in post–Cold War postcolonial East Asia. To this end, this chapter examines two texts—the Japanese novelist Tsushima Yūko's *Exceedingly Barbaric* (2008) and the Taiwan aboriginal filmmaker Laha Mebow (Chen Chieh-yao)'s *Finding Sayun* (2010)—as rehabilitations of colonial wounds not through the normative politics of recognition, but a fictive articulation of intergenerational intimacy through indigenous knowledge of myth-making that displaces historical colonialism as the primary site where an alternate and nonstatist reconciliation can take place.[1]

Taiwan in East Asian Historical Reconciliation

China's rise is seriously challenging the postwar–Cold War system orchestrated and dominated by Japan and its American ally in the region. Neoliberal policies of varying forms and degrees have brought about economic instability and social anxiety—a general sense of precarity—especially among the youth and the underclass. The resort to nationalist sentiment and chauvinistic negativity has increased, along with the desire to address historical issues of Japanese colonialism and imperialism and the destructive violence and pain it has inflicted on the neighboring countries. While much of the wrangling is performed by the state that fastidiously fans or foils nationalist fervors among its citizens for its political means, there have been collaborations among scholars aimed at transcending national history and at crafting a regional, if not global, history based on mutual agreement. However, even with this laudable effort, Taiwan, as a participant and object of inquiry, is surreptitiously left out. Debates on past conflicts and their resolution in the region are often depicted as that between Japan and South Korea, or Japan and China, leaving Taiwan, Japan's colony for fifty years, not to mention Hokkaido and the Ryūkyūs, Japan's initial colonies, outside of current discussions. For example, the Common History Project, a trilateral joint history editorial committee formed of mostly historians from South Korea, China, and Japan, has published thus far two collections: *A History That Opens to the Future: The Contemporary and Modern History of the Three East Asian Countries* (2006) and *New Modern History of East Asia, Vol. 1: Reading Changes in International Relations* (2012a), and *Vol. 2: People and Exchanges* (2012b).

The attempt by these scholars to forge a transnational history of the region beyond national history is indeed commendable and desirable. However, the almost complete exclusion of one of Japan's most important colonies is curious if not baffling. (The only place Taiwan is mentioned is in the second volume of *New Modern History of East Asia* under the theme "Railroads.") The exclusion of Taiwan from the Common History Project publications can be attributed to Taiwan's lack of nation-state status in the negotiations among so-called sovereign states. However, if the project is to rewrite regional history, then why insist on the dominant configuration of the nation-state form? Besides Taiwan's lack of independence, I surmise that the preclusion is also based on the assumption that Taiwan has nothing to offer in a history-writing project with an aim toward reconciliation. Hence, the project is symptomatic of contemporary political negotiation between the three nation-states rather than a thorough rewriting of regional and transnational history that can transcend national(ist) histories. Taiwan is excluded because it is perceived NOT to be in conflict with Japan over past history the ways South Korea and China are, despite the facts that Taiwan also has claims on the disputed Diaoyu/Senkaku islands and that women from Taiwan were also forced into sex slavery for the Japanese military.

The perceived nonconflicting relationship between Taiwan and Japan results from two independent but interrelated events. First, there is Chiang Kai-shek's "benevolent" gesture of "repay injury with kindness," a conditional and calculated "forgiveness" that supposedly absolved Japanese responsibility not only in Taiwan but also for mainland China. Its aim paralleled American postwar policy to reconstruct and rehabilitate Japan as the primary bastion against rising communist threat in Asia. Second, unlike South Korea and China, with their strong anti-Japanese sentiment, Taiwan was perceived to be "pro-Japanese." This "intimate" relationship is often cited by Japanese conservatives as reflecting the achievements of Japanese colonial rule and juxtaposed against the insidious and grudging Koreans and Chinese. However, as I have argued elsewhere, the "intimacy" between Taiwan and Japan, especially among the generation of *benshengren* who experienced both Japanese and Kuomintang (KMT) rules, has less to do with colonialism itself but more to do with the "postcolonial colonization" of Taiwan by the Nationalist government led by the dictator Chiang Kai-shek himself. The intimacy toward Japan is a decidedly postcolonial phenomenon that reflects more on the oppressive KMT rule than the beneficent Japanese colonialism (Ching 2012). What I want to challenge is the assumption that "intimacy," especially that of a (post)colonial kind, is both a perversion from the normative process of political engagement over conflicts and a betrayal of anti-imperialist nationalism that is not worthy of consideration in the process of reconciliation. The binarisms between resistance and collaboration, enmity and intimacy, need to be rethought in their constitutive, rather than antagonistic, relationship. Taiwan's alleged intimacy with Japan, I suggest, offers the possibility of imagining reconciliation of a different kind.

Theorizing Intimacy

Recent scholarship in critical colonial studies has argued for the complexity, contradiction, ambivalence, and incompleteness of colonial rule. Moving away from the Manichean division of the colonial world, these analyses pay close attention to colonial-subject formation, for both colonized and the colonizer (and their internalization and mutuality), despite the very real violence and subjugation that operate between them. One of the more fecund areas of research is the connection between the broad-scale dynamics (or macro-politics) of colonial rule and the intimate sites of its implementation, or what Ann Stoler has called, following Foucault, the "microphysics of colonial rule" and "the affective grid of colonial politics" (2002: 7). Stoler defines intimacy in this way: "The notion of the 'intimate' is a descriptive marker of the familiar and the essential *and* of relations grounded in sex. It is 'sexual relations' and 'familiarity' taken as an 'indirect sign' of what is racially 'innermost' that locates intimacy so strategically in imperial politics and why colonial administrations worried over its consequence and course" (9). However, as Lisa Lowe (2006) has shown, "intimacy" can be expanded to larger historical and continental connectivities. Beyond domesticity, in both bourgeois and colonial contexts, Lowe's "multivalent of intimacy" also includes "spatial proximity or adjacent connection," where slave societies engendered profits that gave rise to bourgeois republican states in Europe and North America, and the colonial labor relations on the plantations in the Americas also became "the conditions of possibility for European philosophy to think the universality of human freedom, however much freedom for colonized peoples was precisely foreclosed within that philosophy" (193). Intimacies under colonial rule were "embodied in the variety of contacts among slaves, indentured persons, and mixed-blood free peoples" that were eschewed by the colonial management in fear of possible rebellions against the plantation structure itself (203).

In the context of East Asia, the notion of intimacy has formed the basis of Japan's colonial desire and informed its postcolonial entanglement. From the notion of *naisen ittai* (Japan and Korea share one body) and *naitai yūwa* (harmony between Japan and Taiwan) to the contentious category of *shin nichi* (pro-Japan, or intimacy with Japan) and the Greater East Asia Co-prosperity Sphere, the emphasis on the affective union between the colonizer and the colonized has been part and parcel of the Japanese colonial ideology of assimilation and imperialization. In Taiwan's case, the intermarriages between Japanese policemen and daughters of aboriginal tribal leaders are examples of colonialism's "sexual diplomacy." Shōji Sōichi's novel, *Madame Chen* (1940), depicts the marrying of a Japanese woman into a prominent Taiwanese extended family whereby the Japanese woman, enduring hardship and prejudice by the Taiwanese, succeeds in transforming the Chen family into an emperor-worshipping, empire-dedicated household. In postcolonial times, to be "pro-Japan" was to be labeled as a "collaborator" and "traitor" as opposed to the postindependent nationalist discourse of "resistance" and "patriots." In this regard, the "enslaved mentality" of the Taiwanese under Japanese rule entailed the forced "re-Sinicization" by the takeover KMT regime that reproduced the colonial binaries of "Taiwan" and "China," "*benshengren*" and "*waishengren*" with the former deemed inauthentic, perverted, foreign, and hence potentially subversive. The postwar postcolonial Chinese authoritarian rule has propelled many Taiwanese to feeling nostalgic for Japanese rule, lamenting the decline of Japan and stressing over the ascendant Chinese power (Ching 2010).

As mentioned earlier, Taiwan is excluded from the regional discussion of reconciliation because of its alleged intimate relation with Japan. This political and conditional process of reconciliation seems to work from the process of conflict → antagonism → reconciliation that prioritizes differences and incommensurability. Given the violence of Japanese colonialism and imperialism inflicted on its neighbors, this is understandable. However, what if we do not assume that reconciliation must have its prerequisite in antagonism, but that intimacy between the former colonizer and colonized can result in reconciliation (perhaps not the political and normative kind, but on a more interpersonal and intergenerational level)? For the rest of the chapter, I analyze the works by Tsushima and Mebow to explore how intimacy and indigeneity open up a space of reconciliation, not with the colonial past, as normative political processes are prone to do, but with the future, for the unborn and the yet-to-come.

Musha and Sayun

Tsushima's *Exceedingly Barbaric* and Mebow's *Finding Sayun* take as their subjects arguably the two most important and interrelated historical events concerning Taiwanese aborigines during the Japanese colonial period: the Musha Rebellion and the Bell of Sayun, respectively.[2] My choice of these two texts as exemplars of what I am calling "reconciliation otherwise" is based on their departure from the normative accounts on the two events. Although Tsushima's novel recounts the aboriginal killings of Japanese settlers and indicts the savagery of Japanese colonialism and modernity in general, the main concern is the storytelling about a complex psychological conflict and the corporeal desire of Miicha, a Japanese woman trapped in colonial domesticity in 1930s Taipei. Her story is recounted and paralleled by her niece, Lily, who travels to Taiwan in 2005 to retrace her aunt's footsteps.

For Mebow, her film's initial intention to find the "truth" of the story of the sacrificing aborigine girl, Sayun, proved to be futile, and what emerges instead is the relationship between Grandpa, Ah Gong, eager to revisit the forsaken aborigine village and his filial grandson, You-Gan, who accompanies him on the treacherous return. Their respective loci of enunciation are also important. Tsushima, a well-known writer, has, since the mid-1990s, written novels that address Japan's imperial past and war trauma, often dealing with marginal characters and suppressed events. Her concern has always been about women's desire, the experience of losing a child, and patriarchal oppression within Japanese society. *Exceedingly Barbaric* is narrated from the Japanese women's perspectives, and, more specifically, from that of a colonial settler and her niece, whose alternating timelines reveal the asphyxiation of colonial domesticity and the openness of indigenous landscapes. Mebow is the first aborigine woman (from the Atayal tribe) to direct a feature film. As she remarks in an interview, her concern is the disappearing Atayal tradition and culture, which she wants to pass on to the future generation. It is the common concern for futurity—responsibility beyond the now—in the name of the lost child and those yet to be born for Tsushima, and intergenerational connectivity to the ancestors for Mebow, a shift from colonial to familial intimacy that allows for a positive contrapuntal reading of the two texts.

Let me briefly recount the two colonial events concerning the Taiwanese aborigines. The Musha Rebellion was an October 1930 clandestine killing of 134 Japanese, including women and children, by the Seediq indigenous people, making this the largest and most notorious uprising against the Japanese in the country's colonial history. The incredulity and agitation caused by the insurgence consumed the colonial authority to the extent that the subsequent subjugation campaign mobilized approximately three thousand military and police forces (against three hundred rebels) that deployed internationally banned poisonous gas with the clear aim of decimating the rebelling population. While the killing of the Japanese settlers, including women and children, shocked the colonial administration and the public, the sheer barbarity and calculated vengeance against the aborigines shattered the idealized images of compliant natives and benevolent colonizers and crushed the dubious boundary between savagery/civility and barbarity/modernity. The Musha Rebellion is also the subject of a recent blockbuster film in Taiwan. The two-part, four-hour-plus epic *Warriors of the Rainbow: Seediq Bale* (2011), stays relatively faithful to the generally accepted historical narrative, and, unlike Tsushima's novel, represents a masculinist representation of aborigine bravery and violence.[3]

The story of Sayun (or Sayon), or rather the Bell of Sayun in its most popular colonial representation, dramatizes the aboriginal redemption and devotion to the Japanese nation through self-annihilation in the wake of the Musha Rebellion. The Bell of Sayun is the story of Sayun, a seventeen-year-old aborigine woman from the Ryōhen settlement (where Mebow hails from). In September 1938, with the escalating Japanese war in China, Takita, a police officer cum schoolteacher, is drafted to the front. Sayun, with ten other classmates, is to carry the departing officer's luggage to the foot of the mountain. The entourage descends the precipitous mountain path, thirty-four kilometers long, amid a torrential typhoon. As they cross the rising water on the makeshift log bridge, Sayun slips and is swept away by the rapid current. Even after many diligent searches, Sayun's body is never recovered.

Sayun's accident was only casually mentioned in the *Taiwan Daily News* in its September 29, 1938, edition, with the simple heading "Aborigine Woman Missing after Falling into Stream." For three years the story of a drowned seventeen-year-old remained obscure and insignificant. In the spring of 1941, after learning about Sayun's good deed, Governor-General Hasegawa Kiyoshi presented the Ryōhen settlement with a bell inscribed with the following phrase: "The Bell of the Patriotic Maiden Sayun." The commemoration reverberated throughout the island, especially among the aborigines, and generated a media sensation with a number of paintings of Sayun, a popular song, and eventually a film based on her story.

As I have argued elsewhere, the two events are interrelated in what I call "savage construction and civility making" in the Japanese empire (Ching 2001). After the Musha Rebellion, we encounter a visible shift in aborigine representations in the circulation of the culture of colonialism. The aborigines are no longer the savage heathens waiting to be civilized though colonial benevolence; they are imperial subjects assimilated into the Japanese national polity through the expressions of their loyalty to the emperor. In this regard, "Sayun" constitutes a post-Musha tactic of idealizing primitivity in the making of civility. Sayun dramatizes the aboriginal redemption and devotion to the Japanese nation through self-annihilation—a transfiguration from a rebellious savage to a patriotic imperial subject. In other words, Sayun represents a compensation for Musha, as a "rehabilitation" and "redemption" for the violence and evil of the Musha massacre. The barbarity of Musha is "healed" by the patriotism/civility of Sayun. The two events continue to be of interest to writers and filmmakers alike, I propose, precisely because of the contradictions and the mysteries that the colonial narrative generates. How do we reconcile the savage imaginary of the Musha Rebellion with the patriotic endeavor of Sayun? What I would like to suggest through my analyses of *Exceedingly Barbaric* and *Finding Sayun* is that the two texts undermine the colonial narrative at the same time that they construct a postcolonial futurity that opens up a space of hope beyond colonialism's encompassing power.

Displacing Colonialism and Rearticulating Intimacy

Despite their different loci of enunciation—Tsushima from the metropolitan Japanese perspective and Mebow from the Taiwanese aboriginal perspective—they speak from similar subaltern positions vis-à-vis their respective dominant sociohistorical contexts. Tsushima attempts to recount the marginal lives of Japanese women entrapped in colonial domesticity and their liminality between the colonizers and the colonized. As Stoler and others have shown in the Dutch, French, and British imperial cultures, women in the colonies experienced "the cleavages of racial dominance and internal social distinctions very differently than men precisely because of their ambiguous positions, as both subordinates in colonial hierarchies and as agents of empire in their own right" (2002: 41). Tsushima's work certainly points to the ambiguity of Japanese women's experience in settler colonialism: they are confined in the Japanese community and prohibited to travel, but they are provided with domestic helpers from both mainland Japan and the local community; one character assists with her husband's translation of the works of Durkheim (but without official acknowledgment) and endures the husband's demand for intercourse after losing her baby.

As mentioned earlier, *Finding Sayun* is Mebow's first feature film, and as the title in Chinese, *Buyiyang de yueguang* (A different moonlight) suggests, Mebow wants the aborigine community to shine under a different glow. Against the normative filmic depictions of aborigines struggling in urban settings, which often leaves the audience with a heavy heart, Mebow wants to "depict aborigine life through a lighthearted, natural way" (Huang 2011).[4] Using a film within film as a visual prop and the story of Sayun as a narrative device, Mebow takes the audience along with the Atayal people back to the old village, and, more importantly, through the grandfather's elocution, discovers the Atayal people's intimate connection to the ancestors and their land. Based on her own experience of returning to the ancestral village, now barely recognizable as it is depicted in the film, Mebow utilizes aboriginal art and props and had casted mostly aborigine actors and allowed some to ad lib in order to express a natural and "authentic" representation of their lives. In both cases, while colonial history—the Musha Rebellion and the Bell of Sayun—looms large, the novel and the film manage to deflect normative colonial discourse and attempt new storytelling about indigenous experiences that have been marginalized in dominant narratives of colonialism.

The displacement of the dominant colonial narrative allows Tsushima and Mebow to focus on the intimate relationship of the subaltern subjects that, in the final instances, enables alternative forms of reconciliation with the past. Both narratives are initially motivated by the desire to trace the colonial past but end up forging ahead of what is possible in the future. In *Exceedingly Barbaric*, Tsushima initially depicts both Miicha's journey to the colony and her intimate relationship with her husband as romantic and sensual. With the ensuing realization of colonial and domestic oppression culminated by the news of the Musha Rebellion, Miicha begins to identify with Mona Rudao, the Atayal chieftain responsible for the uprising, and to distance herself physically and emotionally from her husband. Toward the end of the novel, Lily ventures beyond what her aunt Miicha could have only dreamed of, to exit the Japanese settlement and leave new tracks in areas where a colonial woman would not have been allowed to venture, especially the central mountain region. Through her encounters with an aborigine elder woman and a Taiwanese man, Lily imagines what Miicha would have experienced if she had been able to travel in the colony. The TV crew's initial attempt to trace the "truth" of Sayun's story ends in futility but is instead rewarded after following Grandpa's trail back to the abandoned old village. In the novel, the two temporalities converge at the end, where the differences between Lily and Miicha become indistinguishable, collapsing colonialism and the Musha Rebellion into the postcolonial present whereby Lily meets and forges an alliance with Mona Rudao, Tewas (his sister), and a contemporary aborigine woman and Taiwanese man in the mountains. The film ends with a series of interviews with the villagers about what they know about Sayun and the drowning incident. What is rendered through these interviews is the impossibility of the "truth" of Sayun. From Sayun's age, the number of students accompanying the teacher descending the mountain, to whether Sayun's action was voluntary or obligatory or whether her relationship to the teacher was amorous or not, the villagers' opinions are divergent and contradictory. The main reason for the incertitude is that there are no surviving witnesses, including

Sayun's classmates who joined her on the descent. The colonial trace, much like the Derridean trace, marks the presence but suppressed nonpresence of colonialism: the oppressiveness of colonial domesticity erases the aboriginal worldview of myth-making and enchantment. Hence, tracing is not a dutiful reproduction of the past (because the past is always shifting and open to interpretation), but a path to a new vista for reconciliation, not with colonialism at large but with family members and intimate others.

Much of Miicha's life and thoughts are narrated through her niece. Lily's travel to central Taiwan, seventy-some years after Miicha's death, is recounted in the form of dreams, personal reflections, and speculations. Soon we find that Lily not only resembles her aunt, but also had lost her eleven-year-old son during a traffic accident, just as Miicha lost her infant child in colonial Taiwan. Part of Lily's trip to Taiwan, besides wanting to find out how her aunt lived during the colonial period, is to alleviate her pain (or to "wait it out," as she puts it) from the loss. In fact, it is through Lily's travel to the mountains, her encounters with an elderly aboriginal woman and Mr. Yang, a Taiwanese man who accompanies Lily on her travels, that we learn much about aborigine legends and customs, such as the "cloud leopard" and "the yellow butterflies" that construct an alternate world of spirituality and mythology.

Toward the end of the novel, the two temporalities merge as Miicha's and Lily's worlds converge in a dream sequence: "Is this Lily's dream or Miicha's dream? They're the same. It is impossible to separate Lily's dream from Miicha's. There is no reason to distinguish them" (334). Lily and Miicha are joined by Mr. Yang, who could be Mona Rudao, Tewas, and Meimei, the young Taiwanese helper who died at the age of fifteen. What is shared by them is the intimate loss of a young life. Each carries a baby on his or her back. The figures are accompanied by a black dog, with a shadow of the "cloud leopard" for their journey to "fix the world" burning with three suns. The three suns story refers to the popular aborigine mythology of the human effort to eliminate the extra sun (told earlier in the novel). Because the suns are far away from the human realm, the aboriginal myth has each member of the entourage accompanied by young babies as they embark on the long journey to where the suns rest. By the time the group of strong and young men reaches the suns, they have become old and feeble. However, the young babies have grown and are now capable of striking down the extra sun. Once the extra sun has been eliminated and the world returns to its normal order, the young men begin their journey back home. By the time they arrive home, they become old themselves. Lily and her group will repeat this journey but with three suns instead of two. (Could the extra sun be a reference to Japan?) Intimacy here is bounded by the living, the dead, and the yet to come. According to the novel, the entourage does not have to be people from the same nation, tribe, or race, and the babies they carry do not have to be blood-related. They resemble what Lowe has called "the volatile contacts of colonized peoples" (203). What they share are a sense of loss and a task to forge forward to "fix this world." More important, to accomplish or to right the world requires an intergenerational effort that links the young and transcends divisions between colonizers/colonized, *naichi* (mainland Japan)/*gaichi* (overseas territory), and the dead/the living.

The prologue at the beginning of *Finding Sayun* foretells not only the impossibility of finding the "truth" about Sayun, but also a hint at a different path to be followed. The film begins with Li Ke-xiao's reflection: "There is a big difference between the worlds of reality and the novel, but I don't want to listen to the recordings of truth. It is just like I did not begin this road of discovery for the truth of Sayun." The search for the truth regarding Sayun's story (a colonial narrative) turns out to be a failed endeavor, especially the "intimate" relation between the Japanese teacher and the young aborigine girl. In the end, there are only multiple narratives about what "really" happened. In the process of searching for the truth about Sayun, we are led instead to the relationship between You-Gan and Grandpa, Grandpa and the ancestors, the "old village" and the spiritual world of reciprocity. Whereas Tsushima imagines a more cosmopolitan mode of belonging based on shared losses, Mebow's concern is more local and specific to her people. Along the treks to the mountains, Grandpa is seen joyously singing Japanese songs, mostly about missing loved ones. However, Grandpa's affection here is directed toward the prospect of seeing the old village than toward nostalgia for the colonial period. Intimacy here shifts from the colonial love between teacher and Sayun (indeterminacy) to that of an alleged young love between Grandpa and Sayun (fabrication) and finally to that between Grandpa, the younger generation, and ancestors (indigenous knowledge). In arguably the most poignant scene in the film, Grandpa and the entourage reach the old village in what looks like nothing but landscape filled with piles of dirt and weeds. Upon locating what he believes is the site of his ancestral home, Grandpa begins to speak. Alternating between close-ups of an emotional Grandpa with You-Gan holding him and medium shots of the mountainous landscape,

Grandpa first speaks about the unconditional love between his parents and him and the debt he owes to them: "Dad, Mom, without you, I won't exist today. It's you who raised me. If you hadn't raise me and teach me, I wouldn't have grown up, and I wouldn't be standing here." Moving then from the personal, the familial, to the communal, grandfather laments: "Many tribal people want to come up here. All the tribal people make efforts to come up here. Everyone misses here [he sobs]. Everyone wants to come back here to see the original state of the tribe. Maybe this is the last time I come back. I can't see you. But instead in front of you I shed my tears. Do you hear me? I never cry like this. Because I really miss you and your homeland." You-Gan then embraces Grandpa.

The Taiwanese crew then asks the younger generation, You-Gan and his friend A-Guo, what they think about the old village and Grandpa's emotional connection to it. You-Gan responds: "I haven't lived there, so I don't feel much. If I had, and then saw my hometown ruined like this . . . I might cry like him." A-Guo also empathizes: "I think it's very worthy." "But there is nothing," the reporter retorts. A-Guo continues, "But still . . . I know the ancestral spirits could see me. No matter where I am. I know they can see me." In short, even for the younger generation, despite the ruination of the old village due to the forced relocation policy of the KMT, the connection to the past remains imaginable. Mediated through memories of the elders and aboriginal practices of hunting, the tribal lives do not simply vanish due to modernization. The film ends with You-Gan running, not away from the camera as he did at the beginning of the film but forward, toward the future, and the following words are superimposed on the screen: "The mythologies and cultures of the tribal people are slowly disappearing. But my people, whether they're dwelling in the mountains or in the plains, they're continuing to make a great effort to live."

Both Tsushima and Mebow displace colonialism and explore intergenerational reconciliation: between Lily and Miicha, between You-Gan and Grandpa. The displacement of colonialism as a site of reconciliation with the state does not mean disregarding the colonial wound. First, it means to heed the warning of Arif Dirlik (2002) that the obsession with the colonial past runs the risk of obscuring from us the need to confront the changing power relations in the present. This is most obvious in what William Callahan (2010) has called "the discourse of national humiliation" in China, whereby historical defeats and victimization are channeled into nationalist discourse that not only justifies China's return to its imperial grandeur but also obfuscates the contradictions resulting from its uneven development. Second, the demands for reparation and genuine apology from the former colonized have been met with consternation if not outright denial by the Japanese state. The so-called comfort women from South Korea have held weekly Wednesday demonstrations in front of the Japanese embassy since the late 1990s, and many of them have perished while the Japanese state continues to refuse to meet their demands or acknowledge the imperial state's role (and, by implication, the Showa emperor's responsibility) in instituting systemic sex slavery. Caught between the double blackmail of nationalism and colonialism orchestrated by the state, political reconciliation continues to elude and marginalize the very subjects that it purports to represent. It is under this specific historical condition of political impasse that the works of Tsushima and Mebow allow us to imagine different forms of rapprochement outside of state power.

Conclusion

In "On Forgiveness," Jacques Derrida observes that since the Second World War and accelerating in recent years, there has been a "globalization of forgiveness" on the geopolitical scene. In all the scenes of repentance, confession, forgiveness, and apology, "one sees not only individuals, but also entire communities, professional corporations, the representatives of ecclesiastical hierarchies, sovereigns, and heads of state ask for 'forgiveness'" (2001: 28). The concept of forgiveness, the scene, the figure, the language which one tries to adapt to it, argues Derrida, all belong to the Abrahamic tradition and is expanding to cultures that do not have a European or "biblical" origin. To emphasize the universalization of forgiveness in the non-Abrahamic tradition, Derrida uses the example of a Japanese prime minister asking for forgiveness of the Koreans and the Chinese for past violence. Derrida writes, "[The prime minister] presented certain 'heart-felt apologies' in his own name, [at first sight] without implicating the Emperor as the head of state, but a Prime Minister always implicates more than a private person. Recently, there have been real negotiations, this time official and serious, between the Japanese and the South Korean government on this subject. There will be reparations and a political reorientation" (31).[5]

Leaving aside Derrida's contention that the concept of forgiveness is foreign to cultures of Japan or Korea, he points to the "instrumentality" of such apologetic gestures. Derrida continues: "These negotiations, as is almost always the case, aimed at producing a reconciliation (national or international) favorable to normalization. The language of forgiveness, at the service of determined finalities, was anything but pure and disinterested. Always in the field of politics" (31). Derrida is therefore critical of the political appropriation that sidesteps rather than upholds justice in the name of reconciliation. It is in this regard that Derrida sees reconciliation as important, but vested in strategic or political calculation in the generous gesture of one who offers reconciliation or amnesty, but we should not take them to be the same as forgiveness.

What I have explored through these two texts then is the possibility of reconciliation without state intervention or normalization. This is not to diminish the necessary task of holding the Japanese state accountable for its colonial violence and war crimes. Because colonial rule and war are waged in the name of the state and the emperor, any gesture toward reconciliation and forgiveness has to begin with their admission and indictment. However, with shifting geopolitical power in Eastern Asia and the rising tension among nation-states, it is unlikely that a reconciliation beyond any categorical imperative, beyond any debt and obligation, is possible in the near future. Even if some agreement is reached between the states, the conditions attached to such will only serve to reestablish national and political (hetero)normativity, such as the 2015 accord between Japan and South Korea on the comfort women issue. Equally important, the last generation that experienced colonial rule and war is fast disappearing. Their demands for apologies and reparation and their yearning for recognition have been largely ignored by the Japanese, Taiwanese, and Korean states. I am interested in ways that people today, who lived through colonial rule or were born in the postcolonial present, come to terms with their memories of colonialism.

Derrida's caution on reconciliation's conditional instrumentalism is echoed by others. In a scathing critique of a photo essay published by the *New York Times* that commemorated the twentieth anniversary of the Rwandan genocide, Suchitra Vijayan (2014) problematizes the very narrative of reconciliation, forgiveness, and transformation that not only simplifies the complexity of the killings and its aftermath, but also obfuscates the violence perpetrated by the state in the name of reconciliation. Vijayan first takes issue with the single "overarching identity" that subsumes the other fractured and contradictory Rwandan identities into simple "binary preoccupations between Hutu and Tutsi, Good and Evil, Victim and

Perpetrator, and Redemption and Liberation." This simplification is reinforced by a series of photographic images of a Hutu and a Tutsi, side by side, with brief testimonies recounting their requests for forgiveness and decisions granting forgiveness, respectively. These feel-good stories of redemption do not confront the more difficult questions of moral ambiguities where victims become perpetrators, or the strife of living with irresolvable conflicts. Reconciliation "immediately becomes complicit in the exercise of various forms of structural violence in its appeal to an idea of commonality to legitimate a social hierarchy."

The photo essay also fails to account for the Rwandan state's refusal to prosecute alleged war crimes committed by the Rwandan Patriotic Army and associated individuals before, during, and after the genocide, including retribution killings of thousands of Hutu. The simplified narrative of incommensurable Hutu guilt and Tutsi victimhood formed the foundation of postgenocide Rwandan political power. The memory of the genocide is therefore instrumentalized to stifle dissent and international criticism, and the act of reconciliation, "although sometimes genuinely participatory, has been manipulated to intimidate Kagame's political opponents and consolidate power." As Vijayan argues, the demand for forgiveness and the extraction for reconciliation ultimately serve the calculus and imperative of the state into what Derrida calls "national reconciliation" (40). These conditional reconciliations, although necessary and important, would not achieve intended goals without the radical reorganization of power.

At the end of his rumination on forgiveness, Derrida dreams of the "purity" of a forgiveness worthy of its name. It would be "a forgiveness without power: unconditional but without sovereignty." The most difficult task, he continues, "at once necessary and apparently impossible, would be to dissociate unconditionality and sovereignty" (59). How to imagine nonsovereign social and subjective formations in political discourse also preoccupy theorists such as Michael Hardt and Lauren Berlant in their use of the idiom of love as a political concept. Despite their theoretical differences, they both view love as transformative, collective, and sustainable (Davis and Sarlin 2008). While not addressing the specific issue of true forgiveness or love as a nonsovereign possibility of the social, my uses of sentimentality and reconciliation in these chapters are attempts to imagine a nonstatist, noncolonial, and nonguaranteed working-out of historical injustice and colonial memories. In this transimperial moment in the region—the decline of Japan and the rise of China and its unresolved colonial past and unsettling globalizing present—we must attend to the legitimate resistance to colonialism without obscuring its entanglements with the very real competition for hegemony in East Asia today. Anti- and pro-Japanese sentiments, as I have argued throughout the book, are symptoms of the failure of the decolonization of the Japanese empire and the reemergence of China under global capitalism. The competition for economic accumulation and political authority under the Borromean knot of nation, state, and capital will render Derrida's dream of "unconditional and non-sovereign forgiveness" unlikely in the foreseeable future.

Transimperial figures such as the repentant former Japanese devils, the recalcitrant comfort women, the nostalgic *dōsan* generation, and the affectionate aboriginal elders all straddle the imperial divide between Japanese empire and the postwar Cold War order. As many people perish due to the passage of time, their struggle, resolve, resentment, and longing are testament to the failure of postcolonial nation-states to critically confront and address issues of responsibilities, reparation, and redress. No doubt there will be attempts at conditional reconciliation, such as the Japan–South Korea accord over the comfort women issue (see chapter 3) as states become eager to facilitate economic and cultural exchanges through political means. At the same time, competing nationalism will be mobilized to assuage internal contradictions by constructing and recalling past atrocities and inflicted pains. The liberal discourse of reconciliation and the nationalist discourse of redemption are not mutually exclusive and are in fact symptoms of the same process of neoliberalist capitalism. In this regard, the nation-state cannot be counted on as the space for unconditional reconciliation, for its basic mode of operation is conditional negotiation. To overcome anti- and pro-Japanism is therefore to explore trans- and subnational forms of affiliations and to imagine reconciliation otherwise.

EPILOGUE. From Anti-Japanism
to Decolonizing Democracy:
Youth Protests in East Asia

Democracy is hypocrisy.
—MALCOLM X

Between March 2014 and August 2015, major student-led demonstrations erupted throughout East Asia. The Sunflower and the Umbrella movements and protests led by Students Emergency Actions for Liberal Democracy (SEALDs) drew tens of thousands of people to the streets, objecting to government conduct in Taiwan, Hong Kong, and Japan. Unlike the anti-Japanese protests in major cities in China in 2005 and 2012, the images of young people showed them defiantly occupying public spaces, rallying the crowd with emotive speeches. and sometimes clashing with police. Also, the oft-reported postdemonstration cleanups impressed the general population with the students' exuberance and idealism, seemingly marking the dawn of a new era of democracy in the region. In the name of liberal democracy, these movements seem to have transcended the jingoistic rhetoric and violent display of the anti-Japan demonstrations on the Chinese mainland and elsewhere. While each movement emerged from its particular sociopolitical context, they also resonated with each other in their demands for change and shared tactics, inspired by worldwide youth activism since 2011, especially the Occupy movements. The simultaneity of local, national, regional, and global interconnectedness appears to debunk the perception of political apathy among youths in the region. Many have remarked on the unprecedented use of social media and the seemingly "leaderless" and nonhierarchical organization of current movements. I would like to, however, approach the student protests from a regional perspective and suggest an alternative to anti-Japanism. These movements, despite their different political visions and local circumstances, have the potential to forge transnational and regional political initiatives that can contribute to inter-Asian dialogue and activism. First, I would like to address two characteristics common to the three movements. The first characteristic is the importance of popular culture in providing a common grammar for regional interlocution and inter-referencing. The second characteristic is their shared concern about the rise of China and the general sense of precarity among the youth in the region. Second, I will argue that, without questioning and challenging the complicity of democracy in suppressing the colonial question in the postwar capitalist order, especially in Japan, the movements would not be able to transcend the limits of liberalism and nationalism. In short, what is needed is to shift the discourse from anti-Japanism to the decolonization of democracy.

A 2016 publication written by SEALDs (translated as *Youths Never Give Up—Japan, Hong Kong, and Taiwan: Is a Transnational Student Solidarity Possible?*) features five conversations between members of the organization (Okuda Aki, Ushida Yoshimasa, and Mizoi Moeko) and student activists from Hong Kong (Agnes Chow and Joshua Wong) and Taiwan (Chen Wei-Ting). The question mark in the book title clearly suggests an open-ended project-in-progress without presuppositions and clear objectives. It also underscores the aspiration and adversity of transnational alliance building. Conducted in a free-flowing style and facilitated by an editor, the Japanese youths converse with Wong (in three chapters) and with Chow and Chen (one chapter each) on a variety of topics, ranging from initial impressions of each other's movements and the challenge of balancing dating with activism to more substantial discussions on mobilization tactics and the political visions of poststudent movements. What I want to focus on are two aspects of the conversations that are relevant to an emerging regional sensibility: popular culture as common grammar among the youths, and China as the new hegemon in the region. It is clear from their exchanges that the students have been following each other's activities via social media and express great admiration for one another. The discussions are amicable, jovial, and engaging. There might be minor disagreements regarding future political roles—to form oppositional parties or to continue the struggle from nonestablished political institutions—but the conversations are more about finding commonality than proclaiming differences. What is striking, however, is the sheer ignorance of the Japanese youths toward their Asian neighbors, a process of de-Asianization characterizing Japan's relation to Asia since the postwar years. Ushida, one of the SEALDs members, acknowledges this in the preface. Ushida admits that he, and perhaps most Japanese youths, heretofore have not seriously considered themselves as belonging to the same geo-space that is called "East Asia." While a plethora of images and ideas is circulating on the internet, he expresses the difficulty that Japanese have in imagining how to share this regional space with other youths. Ushida postulates this as simply an observation, but avoids probing into the reasons behind their obtuseness. It is only through their conversations on democracy and political movements that Ushida begins to realize their commonalities and aspirations (10). This self-awareness, however, as I will suggest later, must transform into a decolonizing project of Japanese democracy itself that the youths are trying to salvage. Unbeknownst to Ushida and his colleagues, youths from Hong Kong and Taiwan know much more about Japan than they themselves know about Hong Kong or Taiwan. Japanese popular culture plays an indispensable role in creating and facilitating this transnational imagined community. Agnes Chow, Joshua Wong, and Chen Wei-Ting were all born in the 1990s. This generation's relationship with Japan, especially with its cultural products, is significantly different from their parents' or grandparents' generations, when memories of war and colonialism remain strong. Hong Kong has witnessed an upsurge of interests in Japanese popular culture, especially popular music, in the 1980s and in anime and manga in the 1990s. In post–martial law and market liberalization Taiwan, Japanese popular culture has been favored by young people, known as the *hari-zu*, or "Japan-fever tribe," since the early 2000s. Beyond anime and manga, Japanese TV drama, music, films, cuisine, fashion, literature, and so on have been avidly consumed by youths in Taiwan, Hong Kong, and increasingly China, via the internet. Given the exposure during their formative years, it is not surprising that Chow, Wong, and Chen are all familiar and fluent in Japanese popular culture. What I want to underscore here is that for Chow, Wong, and Chen's generation, "Japan" is no longer external or foreign; Japanese popular culture created intimate objects and texts that are part of their everyday lives. While there are different levels of engagement with Japanese popular culture among the youths, what I am suggesting here is the "quotidian" aspect of cultural practice and consumption. Through popular culture, youths from the three lo-cales can claim a shared time and space where one can reference another via common texts. For example, Wong tells the story that during a debate with one of the parliamentary officials, he used the phrase "we're the cho-sen children" to describe their group. The phrase comes from one of his favorite Japanese anime, *Digimon*. Upon hearing this, Okuda immediately jumps in and says *Digimon* is also one of his favorites and that he still sings the theme song from the anime at karaoke bars. In her conversation, Chow also reveals that she is a big fan of Japanese manga and anime, and she often posts anime songs on her Facebook page. Wong reports being an avid *Gundam* fan. Chen also expresses his liking of Japanese manga and novelists such as Haruki Murakami and Ryū Murakami. He relays how he learned about Japanese social movements from reading nonmain-stream manga such as *Medusa*, depicting the Anpo protests in the 1960s, and *Stories of My Village*, on the Sanrizuka struggle over the construction of Narita Airport in the 1970s. Chen also mentions that Japanese intellec-tuals such as Karatani Kōjin and Oguma Eiji have visited and given talks in Taiwan over the last few years. Compared to Chow, Wong, and Chen's enthusiasm for and knowledge of Japanese popular culture, it is striking that none of the Japanese youths mention even in passing a single cul-tural reference from Taiwan or Hong Kong. This "transnational imagined community" is by no means equal in production, distribution, and con-sumption. Japanese youths know very little about cultures and intellectual developments outside of their archipelago. This emerging shared space of "East Asia" is based on an asymmetrical relationship where Japanese youths have much to learn, especially its colonial and imperialist history in Asia and its postwar postcolonial de-Asianization. To this end, anti- and pro-Japanism are important discourses for Japanese youth to engage with Asia as a starting point toward the decolonialization process.

The second common thread in the conversations is the rise of China and its regional and global implications. Hong Kong and Taiwan, for obvi-ous reasons, have a complicated and constraining relationship with main-land China. However, the way that Japan, as a former colonial power and a staunch ally of the United States, reacted to China's rise (and its own decline) is no less problematic. Chow, Wong, and Chen perceive China as a threat to universal democratic values. They see their political activism and energy as a means of resisting and disrupting the power of Beijing. For Okuda, Ushida, and Mizoi, the Abe administration trumpeted about the Chinese threat as a way to frighten the populace into submitting to the security bills that allowed the state to reinterpret the postwar constitution and deploy military overseas under the vague declaration of a "proactive contribution to peace." While the demand for universal suffrage is considered the main impetus for the Umbrella Movement, it is to protest the directive of "moral and national education" by the Hong Kong government and Beijing in 2012 that Chow and Wong sprang into activism by forming Scholarism. For Chen and the Sunflower Movement, it is the secret passing of the Cross-Strait Service Trade Agreement (CSSTA) by the then-ruling Kuomintang (KMT) Party that provided the movement's impetus. The CSSTA, signed in 2013 but still unratified, aimed to liberalize trade in services between mainland China and Taiwan. Chen also traces the general support for their movement to 2008 when the KMT returned to power under Ma Ying-jeou and his policy of a closer relationship with Beijing. Chen cites a number of pre-Sunflower protests that culminated in the 2014 movement: the 2008 student protest against the visit of Chen Yunlin, chairman of the Association for Relations across the Taiwan Strait, the highest-level meeting in sixty years between the KMT and the Chinese Communist Party; the 2012 student-led Anti-Media Monopoly Movement that rose against media conglomeration and the rhetoric of pro-Chinese national economic development; and the 2013 protests against forced demolition of rural housing. To demonstrate solidarity with Hong Kong and Taiwan colleagues, Okuda says SEALDs has published several statements requesting the Chinese state "understand the values of freedom and democracy" (48). The SEALDs stance against several security-related bills is largely due to the students' objection to the Abe administration's blatant disregard for the constitution. Students against Secret Protection Law (SASPL), a SEALDs predecessor, was formed in opposition to the Special Secrecy Law in 2014. One of the key catalysts behind these bills is Abe's attempt at reviving nationalism by fanning fear and people's anxiety over the rise of China. For the activists, however, it is not so much the content of the bills that is the issue, but the ways in which the ruling party has strong-armed the revisions despite enormous popular opposition.

While the threat of China cannot be understated, I would argue that there's a deeper anxiety over the future of their lives that undergirds the youths' political awakening. It is this shared sense of precarity among youths worldwide that constitutes the core of the problem. What Anne Allison (2013) has perceptively analyzed in the case of precarious Japan is becoming normative in the region and beyond. The anti-China sentiment, like anti-Japanism discussed in the book, is symptomatic of a larger structural shift in the region. Wong describes this global youth problem as that of "exclusion from wealth": low-paying jobs with no prospects (148). The wave of neoliberal policies in the last few decades has increased competition, emphasized individual responsibilities, created more inequality, and blurred young people's visions of the future. It is important to recall here Judith Butler's (2004) differentiation between "precariousness," a general condition for all human existence, and "precarity," a specific condition pertaining to a segment of the population as the result of state policy. I would add that the emergence and resonance of precarity in most developed economies is very much a middle-class phenomenon. This is not to diminish the real challenge faced by young people globally. In the three areas under discussion, there are populations who have always felt the brunt of precarity, such as the aborigines in Taiwan, low-waged laborers in Hong Kong, and resident Koreans in Japan. It is only when the dominant middle class began to feel the pressure and compression from neoliberalism that precarity gained urgency in describing this phenomenon as a specific condition of uncertainty.

These movements are about reforming existing systems, not eliminating them. Part of the desire for direct action (not direct democracy) is the belief in localism/nationalism among the youths. The threat of China prompted Hong Kongers to demand a democratic system and not the official "one-country two systems"; the mainland economic juggernaut has instilled a growing Taiwanese consciousness, the so-called naturally independent, and participation in the political process has made Japanese youths realize if not amplify their sense of national identity. They do, however, distinguish between "good" and "bad" nationalisms. The rise of right-wing populism represented by Marine Le Pen and Donald Trump is considered exclusionary, whereas they see themselves as representing an open and inclusive form of nationalism. Chen even argues that Taiwanese nationalism is distinct for its identification with a place, Taiwan, rather than being based on blood or ethnicity. For them, therefore, democracy and nationalism are complementary.

The unequal relationship between Japan and other Asian spaces, its imperialist past (including unresolved issues such as the "comfort women" and territorial disputes), and its client-state status to that of the United States necessitate serious reflection on the formation of postwar Japanese democracy and its obfuscation of the colonial question. The limitation of SEALDs, I argue, lies in the youths' inattentiveness to the reconfiguration of Japanese empire in the postwar where defeat, demilitarization, and democracy replaced the process of decolonization. SEALDs is a liberal and reformist movement that, due to its massive media coverage and wide support, marginalizes more radical demands. Robin O'Day (2015) has argued that the SEALDs movement, unlike some Freeter activists who call for radical change, attempts to restore the general status quo of the pre-Abe period. (Freeters are young people who lack full-time employment or are un- or underemployed, excluding housewives and students.) However, unlike the issue-focused and media-driven SEALDs, the Freeter movement, short of calling into question the foundations of Japanese postwar capitalism, is not able to identify a cause, event, or action that would address the grievance behind the movement. What the SEALDs phenomenon demonstrates, according to O'Day, is the formation of a new political identity among college students in Japan: social movement is part of their lives but not their whole lives. It is acceptable to seriously engage with political ideas without becoming radical or having to completely devote themselves to the cause. The idea, given Japan's general apathy in the last half-century, is not progressive but resonates with a broad spectrum of students.

Despite large public protests led by SEALDs and other civil groups, the Abe government passed a new set of security bills in September 2015. The main bill allows the country's military to participate in foreign conflicts, overturning its prior policy of self-defense. More specifically, by reinterpreting passages from the Japanese constitution, the legislation allows for the military to operate overseas for the "collective self-defense" of its allies. The government claims that the revision was necessary to meet new geopolitical challenges, such as those posed by China's rising ambitions. However, the new condition that necessitates the security bills goes beyond the region proper. Citing worldwide terrorist threats, it sees security threats to Japan from anywhere in the world. Critics and opponents argue that this violates the constitution and could lead Japan into unnecessary U.S.-led wars abroad. They also charged the Abe administration with destroying Japan's postwar liberal democracy and the ideal of pacifism that that very democracy had established and sustained. It is this opposition to the Abe administration's reinterpretation of the constitution and an undeterred "faith" in postwar democracy that made the question of colonialism invisible.

I argued in chapter 1 that there is a continuity rather than a rupture in Japan's postwar transition and reconstruction from empire and militarism to demilitarization and democracy. Pacifism became one of the pillars (together with capitalism) of Japan's postwar democracy represented by Hiroshima and Nagasaki. The ambiguity of the Hiroshima cenotaph that absolves both the American crimes of dropping the bomb and the Japanese crimes regarding war and colonial responsibilities in Asia. The marginalization of the Korean A-bomb victims and their memorials in the dominant narrative of Japan's victimization conveniently leave out the questions of empire. The architecture of the Hiroshima Memorial Hall was based on the draft design of the Greater East Asian Co-prosperity Hall by Tange Kenzō in the 1940s; the Nagasaki Peace Statue was created by Kitamura Seibō, who created masculinist military sculptures for the Japanese empire. The appeal to world peace and humanism, as universalism often does, conceals its particular enunciation and the colonial difference. That Japan, the only country in history to suffer from nuclear attacks, will not sign the treaty to ban nuclear weapons, adopted at the United Nations and supported by 122 countries, indicates the hypocrisy of pacifism and Japan's continued submission to American hegemony.

Hang Kim (2016) has argued that the belief in constitutionalism and liberal democracy in postwar Japan is based on an "idealism" of world peace by restraining the sovereign power of each nation-state under the guidance of the universal norms (482). It stipulates that the sovereign power of a nation-state should be restrained by a universal norm of international society: the primary presupposition it refers to is not so much a denial of war itself as an inhibition of war between sovereign states. According to that universalism, international conflicts should be resolved by intervention of international organizations such as the League of Nations or the United Nations (483). This universalism, however, enables certain nations to exercise armed forces against ones that commit "crimes against humanity." Once a war is declared in the name of humankind, those opponents cannot but be named "the enemy of all." The figure of the pirate is associated with the enemy of all and thus should be banished from human society and allowed to be exterminated without any consideration of legality. Kim argues that the primary supposition of the postwar Japanese constitution is thus to sanction a universal war, and the newly passed security bills continue to sanction (rather than oppose) the Japanese government in exercising an armed force in the name of international protection.

It is to this adherence to universalism that Kim argues that legislation of the new security bill neither violates nor diverges from the constitution of postwar Japan. He writes,

> Rather, it inherits the spirit of the Constitution. The Japanese government actually denies changes in the basic position of the universalism by placing an emphasis on the expression "Proactive Contribution of Peace." . . . [W]hat the government has done is, if inadvertently, to uncover the hidden legal and political consequence of the universalism that has sustained the postwar democracy and constitutionalism in Japan. Given postwar Japan's support of Americans during the Korean and the Viet Nam wars, the new security bill should be regarded as a declaration that the Japanese government "proactively" inherits the ideal of universalism and continues to support international cooperation in the future. (484)

Therefore, it is not sufficient to criticize the Japanese government's attempt to change the new law of peace and security by upholding postwar democracy and constitutionalism (as SEALDs would claim), because at the very core of those ideals lies the possibility of war against the enemy of all. "It is necessary to reconsider the universalism of the postwar democracy and constitutionalism in Japan, taking into account how and in what way the idea of war against the enemy of all has influenced (the) discourses and thoughts in postwar Japan" (Kim 2016: 484). Kim then proceeds to explicate the interrelationship between the universalism of postwar democracy and colonialism.

Examining the controversy over the publication of Park Yuha's *Comfort Women of the Japanese Empire* and the response by the *zainichi* writer Seo Kyungsik, Kim underscores the elision of colonialism in the establishment of Japanese postwar democracy. Seo's criticism of Park and her Japanese supporters is that their faith in postwar democracy and constitutionalism conveniently ignores the plight of the Korean residents in Japan who were subjects of the empire. (We might also add the Taiwanese, Ainu, and Ryūkyūans to the similar exclusion from democracy.) After Japan's defeat, many of these former subjects had no choice but to remain in Japan. The Japanese government, however, treated these people not as citizens of their country but as foreigners. The former colonial subjects were stripped of their imperial citizenship and deprived of their rights as such. "In this way, the Korean people on the Japanese island after the Second World War lost their legal position as citizens of the country. It is this way that Japanese citizenship after the Second World War has been established; which is to say, the subjects of the postwar democracy of Japan have created their citizenship by excluding the former colonized inhabitants on the island of Japan" (2016: 485). In short, postwar democracy was established by dismissing the responsibility of colonial rule; democracy was established through nondemocratic means.

Kim continues his examination of the relationship between universalism and colonialism through the writing of Nambara Shigeru, one of the most eminent political philosophers and the first president of the University of Tokyo in postwar Japan. Kim argues that Nambara construes the *tennō*, or emperor, as a medium through which the universal principle of humankind and world peace—as stipulated in the new constitution—can be achieved through the national heritage of Japan and the Japanese people. By educating the Japanese people and transforming them into enlightened individuals via the *tennō* as culture, national heritage can achieve universal value because the ideal of world peace could only be realized throughout the efforts and cooperation of all nations (492). The return of Japan to its original and pure state necessitates the exclusion of "external races," which means the former colonized peoples in the empire. Kim concludes that "it might be said that postwar democracy, from its beginning to date, has been relying on the notion of war against the enemy of all, despite its ideas of world peace and elimination of war. This is a peculiar trait that postwar democracy reveals, the trait that the interwoven relation between universalism and colonialism has formed since 1945" (493).

Capitalism and democracy, two pillars of the postwar American hegemonic project, are under duress. Growing inequality, sectarian violence, and ecological crises are prompting many to seek "transition discourses" that call for a significant paradigmatic or civilizational transformation (Escobar 2018). In terms of democracy, theorists such as Jacques Derrida have examined the contradiction between freedom and equality. Instead of deconstructing democracy, which I understand as the West's self-critique, we should begin by analyzing the colonial and neocolonial conditions of democracy and, following Malcolm X, the hypocrisy of democracy. As I argued in this book, anti-Japanism is symptomatic of a larger structural shift in the region, signified by the rise of China and the unresolved imperial and colonial legacies of the Japanese empire. This transimperial moment involves also the decline of American hegemony but with its unrivaled military capability. While China's ambitions cannot be under-estimated, it is imperative that Japan genuinely and seriously engage with its deimperialization process by embracing anti- and pro-Japanism as a platform to begin dialogues with its Asian neighbors toward a possible regional reconciliation for futurity.

1. This information was retrieved from an article published in 2013 by *Offbeat China*: http://offbeatchina.com/700-million-japanese-soldiers-died-in-china-in-2012. The site is no longer available, but an archived view of the article can still be seen on the site's former Facebook page: https://www.facebook.com/hotpotdaily/posts/414540271964283.

2. For a discussion on anti-Japanism in postwar Korea, see Cheong (1991).

3. On January 15, 1974, as Japanese Prime Minister Tanaka Kakuei landed on the last stop of his five-nation, eleven-day "goodwill" visit to Southeast Asia, anti-Japan riots broke out in Jakarta, the sprawling capital of Indonesia. The violence started with the burning of every Japanese automobile within reach of the approximately 100,000 roaming people and quickly mushroomed into sacking and setting fires to stores and businesses that sold Japanese products, especially those owned by overseas Chinese. At the Astra Toyota agency, the entire stock of new cars went up in flames, their fuel tanks exploding with an occasional thud. At the Pasar Senen shopping center, thousands of rioters looted the Chinese-owned stores and stalls and started fires, where seven of the ten known victims of the two-day riots were killed. The Presidential Hotel, operated by Japan Airlines, became the target of the rioters as security forces hurled back wave after wave of rioters with clearly shaken Japanese guests watching fretfully from their windows. The protests and riots were so violent and widespread, Tanaka would be a virtual prisoner in the Dutch-colonial guesthouse within the presidential compound, guarded by hundreds of commando troops and armored vehicles. As with most postwar postcolonial anti-Japanism in Asia, the protests and the ensuing violence are less about Japan than symptoms of contradictions within the Indonesian society. Among the feelings anti-Japanism detonated was outrage over the corruption of government

officials and the ostentatious lifestyle of the rich generals. The students resented the special privileges held by the ethnic Chinese residents; they were also angry that the nation's newfound wealth from oil had not bettered the lives of the Indonesian masses. In short, Tanaka's visit enabled the surfacing onto the symbolic realm the repressed desire and anger of the Indonesian people under continued political authoritarianism and economic disenfranchisement.

4. Dower (2000); Bix (2001).

5. It is important to note here that these "stereotypes" of the Japanese should not be apprehended as simply "negative" or "reductive." These images ultimately create social realities. See Chow (2002), especially chapter 2.

ONE. When Bruce Lee Meets Gojira

1. Throughout the manuscript, I use "Gojira" to refer to the Japanese version of the monster and films and "Godzilla" to refer to its Americanized counterpart. The differentiation is crucial, I argue later on, not only for production purposes, but for politics and the power differential as well.

2. In May 2014, a new Godzilla film directed by Gareth Edwards screened in theaters around the world. While paying homage to the original *Gojira* film and with a visual reference to the Fukushima disaster, the film anthropomorphizes Gojira as a hero fighting off the Mass Unidentified Terrestrial Organisms in order to save the human race. Whereas the original *Gojira* was a warning tale about the nuclear destruction made by humans (or, more specifically, Americans), the newest story absolves humankind of any responsibilities for its destruction of the environment by having Godzilla "balance" nature against the other nuclear-infested monsters. In the succinct words of Professor Serizawa, "Let them fight."

3. My usage of the "postwar Cold War system" requires explanation. It is commonly assumed that "postwar" and "Cold War" share the same time frame: hence, their articulation is redundant and one should use them interchangeably. What gets elided, however, is the "transition" from the ruins of immediate postwar Japan, where political possibilities were denied, if not repressed, with the intensification of the Cold War. In *Democracy and Nationalism*, a comprehensive study of postwar Japanese nationalism and the public sphere, Oguma Eiji (2004) argues that there is not one but two "postwars" in Japanese discourse. The shift from the first to the second postwar, demarcated by the year 1955, witnessed profound changes in discourses about nationalism among the intellectuals. There is the shift from a "developing" to "developed" country, from "Asian" to "Euro-American." There is also the shift from immediate economic deprivation and social disorder to economic recovery, with an emerging consumer society and its affiliated social order and political conservatism. My usage of the "postwar Cold War system" marks and remarks on the transition that bridges the residual elements of Japanese empire with the emergent new nation that vowed to remain pacifist and tied to U.S. hegemony for its economic development.

4. One can also see the catharsis and affective formation of "symbolic anti-Americanism" in postwar popular culture in the personification of Rikidozan and Japanese professional wrestling.

5. For an analysis of Chinese students' activities in the United States and their implications in Asian American politics, see Wang (2013).

6. According to a Wikipedia entry, since 1973 there have been no fewer than four films and eight TV series based on Chen Zhen, Lee's character in *Fist of Fury*.

7. The *Lucky Dragon No. 5* (*Daigo Fukuryū Maru*) incident happened when the Japanese tuna fishing boat of that name was contaminated by a fallout caused by U.S. Castle Bravo thermonuclear weapon test in Bikini Atoll on March 1, 1954. Tudor (1989) defines "secure horror" as structured around clear oppositions. The threat is external. Human action is meaningful. Identification is with the expert. There is an absence of genuine doubt and there is narrative closure.

8. *Enter the Dragon* opened in August 1973 to huge box office returns in the United States. The following February it opened in Hong Kong to much smaller audiences. However, it became a huge hit in Japan, and from 1974 to 1975, three other Bruce Lee films from Hong Kong were screened in Japan.

9. As Yomota (2005) describes it, there were multiple reasons for the delay. First, Raymond Chow, the head of Golden Harvest (a studio in Hong Kong), thought the Japanese were prejudiced against Chinese and Hong Kong people, so he did not consider Japan a viable market. He also did not think the Japanese would take the negative portrayal of the Japanese in *Fist of Fury* very well. From the 1950s to the 1960s, Shaw Brothers and Cathay made films about Japan. Shaw Brothers used Japanese directors and cameramen such as Nakahira Kō (中平康), Inoue Umetsugu (井上梅次), and Nishimoto Tadashi (西本正) to help make action films (17). However, the Japanese film industry showed absolutely no interest in Hong Kong cinema when it was extremely popular in Southeast Asia. Chow was understandably pessimistic about the prospect of exporting Hong Kong cinema to Japan. Second, the Japanese industry had no clue about the influence and reach of Hong Kong cinema in the 1960s. Some socialist films from China were shown, but prejudice against the Chinese was high and so the promoter and distributor wanted to have Bruce Lee scripted in *katakana*—which was associated with foreign loan words in Japanese—instead in Chinese characters. The Japanese came to know Bruce Lee through *katakana* and pronounced his name as "Burusu Li"; South Koreans, by contrast, name Bruce Lee using *hangul* pronunciation, "Yi So Ryon."

TWO. **"Japanese Devils"**

1. This lack of co-evalness with Asia in the postwar Cold War era is similar to the Japanese reception of Bruce Lee (discussed in chapter 1).

2. Sun Ge (2010) gives an example of this *hua-yi* order when Hong Kong was ceded to Great Britain. It was understood by the Qing officials as an act of pacifying the *yi* by the *hua*.

3. I refer here to the textbook controversy of the early 1980s, in which some revisions were made in textbooks for Japanese junior high schools that aimed to minimize the history of Japanese aggression in Asia during the Second World War. The Yasukuni controversy refers to the provocation by Japanese political officials' annual visit to a shrine that worships the war dead.

4. This game can be accessed at http://www.51windows.net/game/index.asp ?fileid=77.

5. This movie can be accessed at http://flash.dm.sohu.com/comic/show_44923 .html.

THREE. Shameful Bodies, Bodily Shame

1. Similar cases of patriarchal nationalism that appropriate and undermine the demands of former comfort women for justice can be seen in the Indonesian case as well. See McGregor (2016).

2. Other than Koreans, women from China, Thailand, French Indochina, Singapore, Malaysia, Burma, Indonesia, the Philippines, and Taiwan were mobilized to serve the Japanese army. For basic facts on the comfort women issue, see "Fact Sheet on Japanese Military 'Comfort Women.'"

3. The situation is the same with other Southeast Asian countries, such as Indonesia. The United States stipulated in Article 14 of the 1951 San Francisco Treaty that Japan should pay "service reparations" to Southeast Asian countries, focusing on the provision of equipment for industrial production rather than monetary payments. The intention of the United States is to help rebuild the Japanese economy to make Japan an Asian regional power that would hold influence over Southeast Asian countries in the context of the Cold War. In 1958 Indonesia signed a treaty with Japan, which included payment of U.S. $223 million over twelve years, the cancellation of trade debt of U.S. $177 million, and $400 million in economic aid. During Suharto's New Order, Japan became one of the biggest contributors of aid and investment in Indonesia. During this time, except for the 1974 anti-Japanese Malari riots over Japanese investment and Indonesian corruption, which were quickly repressed by the military, there was no critical reckoning with the Japanese Occupation or with Japan's ongoing economic influence over Indonesia, not to mention the comfort women issue. See McGregor (2016).

4. See "Treaty on Basic Relations between Japan and the Republic of Korea," *Wikipedia*, accessed August 12, 2012, http://en.wikipedia.org/wiki/Treaty_on _Basic_Relations_between_Japan_and_the_Republic_of_Korea.

5. See also Soyoung Kim's article from 2006, which is a critique of gendered trauma regarding the representation of the Gwangju Uprising. A recent example of the desire to remember and reconstitute the father figure in Korean society is the box office success of *Ode to My Father* (2014; dir. Yoon Je-kyoon). The film chronicles modern Korean history from the 1950 to the present day through the protagonist's personal sacrifice and hard work for his family. The tumultuous history of

Korea is condensed into a few symbolic events: the Hungnam evacuation of 1950, the Korean guest workers in West Germany in the 1960s, the Korean participation in the Vietnam War in the 1970s, and the reunion of separated family members of the Korean War in the early 1980s. Each time, Doek-soo, the eldest son and hence the patriarch of the family, sacrifices himself to protect and take care of the family, as he promised his father when he was lost during the evacuation.

6. For an insightful critique of the discourse of *han* and ethnocentrism, see Jung (2007: 296–332).

7. In *The Murmuring*, one of the women calls their plight "our bitter grudge unresolved."

8. For a concise overview, see Leys (2011).

9. The House of Sharing was founded in June 1992 to provide housing for a number of living comfort women. Buddhist organizations and other social groups provided the funding. See http://www.nanum.org/eng/.

10. Literally, "the fact that I was in this brothel!" Thanks to Hae-Young Kim for the Korean transcription.

11. Hyunah Yang puts it this way: "The project was an apparatus designed to protect Japanese women from the threat of rape by military personnel. Virgin Korean girls were, furthermore, the solution protecting Japanese soldiers from venereal disease, which was regarded as one of the factors weakening military morale and effectiveness" (1997: 63).

12. *Stolen Innocence* is the title of Kang Duk-kyong's painting. The painting depicts a Japanese soldier as a tree, with a naked girl lying at its roots while flowers are falling.

13. The shift from being the object of a film to the subject of filming is further developed in the third documentary, *My Own Breathing* (1999), where Lee Young Soo, a former comfort woman, takes an active role in interviewing other women.

14. For a "revisionist" view of Hirohito's active involvement in the war and its aftermath, see Bix (2001).

15. The judgment is rendered as follows: "The Tribunal finds, based on the evidence before it, that the Prosecution has proved its case against the accused Emperor Hirohito, and finds him guilty of responsibility for rape and sexual slavery as a crime against humanity, under Counts 1–2 of the Common Indictment, and guilty of rape as a crime against humanity under Count 3 of the Common Indictment. Additionally, the Judges determine that the government of Japan has incurred state responsibility, as recognized under Article 4 of the Charter, for its establishment and maintenance of the comfort system."

The Court comprised the distinguished judges Carmen Argibay (Argentina), Christine Chinkin (United Kingdom), and Willy Mutunga (Kenya) and was presided over by the Honorable Judge Gabrielle Kirk McDonald (United States), who delivered the highly anticipated judgment. See http://iccwomen.org/wigjdraft1 /Archives/oldWCGJ/tokyo/index.html.

16. See Choe (2001). The Japanese government officially claimed that the statue

of comfort women breached the Vienna Convention on Diplomatic Relations, an international treaty that outlines a framework for diplomacy.

17. See "Japanese PM Stirs Up Trouble."

18. Nami Kim (2012).

19. Nami Kim (2012).

20. On the issue of political apologies, see Dudden (2014).

21. For the full text of the agreement, see "Japan–South Korea Statement on 'Comfort Women,'" *The Wall Street Journal*, December 28, 2015, http://blogs.wsj .com/japanrealtime/2015/12/28/full-text-japan-south-korea-statement-on-comfort -women/tab/print/.

FOUR. Colonial Nostalgia or Postcolonial Anxiety

1. The previously viewable official page is no longer available. The commission disbanded after four and a half years of classifying all pro-Japanese collaborators and their activities. The effort resulted in a collection of twenty-five volumes, 21,000 pages in all, listing 1,005 collaborators. I would like to thank Lee Hyunjung for translation assistance.

2. The different attitudes of Taiwan and Korea toward Japanese rule can be attributed to a few reasons. First, Korea's precolonial history as a dynastic state within the tributary system of the Chinese empire provided a sense of commonality among its peoples, whereas Taiwan, while a province of the Qing empire, was largely neglected and had little sense of shared belonging. Second, postwar postcolonial occupation by the renegade Nationalist Party significantly impacted the way that Taiwanese people came to compare the two rules. The divided system on the Korean Peninsula and the American Occupation further strengthened Korean nationalism and its shared antipathy to Japanese colonial rule.

3. For a critical analysis of the film, see Chen Kuan-Hsing (2002).

4. *Waishengren* and *benshengren* are categories specific to the postwar Taiwan context. "*Waishengren*," literally, means "people outside of the province," and it refers to those who came to Taiwan from mainland China after the years 1945–49. "*Benshengren*," or "local province people," refers to those who came before 1945–49. These concepts are only meaningful in relation to each other.

5. "*Sakuranohana*" means "cherry blossom."

6. It should be noted that "pro-Japan" (C: *qinri*; K: *chinil*) has very different nuances in Taiwan and Korea. In Taiwan, the term connotes an affinity to Japan or Japanese things; in Korea, the term is used derogatively for collaborators during Japanese rule, especially those branded *chinilpa*.

7. All titles are published by Sakuranohana shuppan (Cherry Blossom Press).

8. The series recently added "testimonies" from Sri Lanka, Indonesia, and the Philippines.

9. The editorial can be found at http://sakuranohana.jp/hokori.html. The assertions cited echo Kobayashi Yoshinori's "comparison" of Japanese colonialism to

Western colonial rule. He categorized Spanish rule in Latin America as a "plundering" type, Britain's rule in India as an "exploiting" type, and Japanese rule in Taiwan and Korea as an "investing" type. See Kobayashi (2000).

10. Quoted in the editorial cited above, available at http://sakuranohana.jp /hokori.html.

11. For an important documentation of this brief period of possibility, see Kō Eitetsu (Huang Yingze) (1999).

12. For the English translation, see Wu and Mentzas (2006).

FIVE. **"In the Name of Love"**

1. "*Cang*" is the mandarin Chinese reading of "*Aoi.*"

2. The political concept of love I am trying to articulate here is different from the "love events" and ultimately heteronormative conceptualization of sexuality and the universalization of the couple implied in Alain Badiou and Nicolas Truong's *In Praise of Love* (2012). Badiou's concern is mainly on the modern romantic love, its inherent and desirable risk (the Encounter), difference (not from the perspective of the One, but of the Two), and points of regeneration. Badiou's commitment to love is to salvage it from the proliferation of technologized and commodified bourgeois relationships.

3. Giddens writes, for example, "Unlike romantic love, confluent love is not necessarily monogamous, in the sense of sexual exclusiveness. What holds the pure relationship together is the acceptance on the part of each partner, 'until further notice,' that each gains sufficient benefit from the relation to make its continuance worthwhile. Sexual exclusiveness here has a role in the relationship to the degree to which the partners mutually deem it desirable or essential" (Kindle loc. 983 of 3627).

4. "*Anpo*" is the Japanese shorthand for the Treaty of Mutual Cooperation and Security between the United States and Japan. The treaty supported the continuous military occupation in Japan, mostly on the island of Okinawa. Despite mass opposition, the treaty was rectified in both 1960 and 1970. For a historical account of the antigovernment art movements, see Marotti (2013).

5. The Komatsugawa Incident refers to the 1958 alleged murder and rape of two Japanese women by an eighteen-year-old resident Korean student, Ri Chin'u.

6. In the film's fifth segment, *R Was Proven to Be a Korean,* although not proven by others, he will accept external confirmation of his Korean identity as a first step toward effectively *becoming* R. The external force is a Korean woman substituting herself for the "corpse" of the schoolgirl who was "strangled" by R. She appears as R's "sister." Initially she is only visible by R and the Education Officer, but later gradually she reveals herself to others as well. One of the significances of this segment is to introduce to the audience the historical oppression of Korean women. "Sister's" logic in trying to convince R to accept himself as R is refuted by the officials and also rejected by R. "Sister" is executed at the end of the segment.

7. The film version, a Chinese, Korean and Japanese coproduction starring Andy Lau and directed by Jacob Cheung, was released in 2006.

8. For a thoughtful critique of state usurpation of the discourse of apologies, see Dudden (2014).

9. Nussbaum writes: "Fraternal sentiment must, in the beginning, be organized at the national level. Unmediated cosmopolitan sympathy for all human beings—'the brotherhood of all, love for all'—is an unrealistic goal at the present time, so immersed are people in egoistic projects and local loyalties. The nation—the democratic nation committed to equal human dignity—is a necessary intermediary between the ego and the whole of humanity: we can already see that the nation can be the object of intense emotions that have motivational efficacy. By building the right sort of patriotism, then, people concerned with universal love may hope to produce the basis for truly international fraternity" (2013: 56).

SIX. **Reconciliation Otherwise**

1. I would like to thank Kerim Friedman for bringing *Finding Sayun* to my attention.

2. I will briefly summarize the texts here. *Exceedingly Barbaric* is a complicated novel narrating the lives of two women—Miicha, a colonial housewife in 1930s Taiwan and Lily, her niece who travels to Taiwan in the summer of 2005 to trace Miicha's footsteps and to alleviate her own sorrow of also losing a child. Alternating between Miicha's letters to Akihiko, her husband; her diaries; and Lily's travelogue, the novel traverses two temporalities—from early 1930s and 2005—to narrate Miicha's life in the colony, with Lily often supplementing Miicha's story through her own narratives. What mediates the two temporalities is the aborigine folklores, beliefs, customs, and, more importantly, the 1930 Musha Rebellion. The notion of barbarity or savagery not only refers to the violent aborigine uprising, the colonial administration's policy or the massive retaliation against the Seediq people, but also serves as a metaphor for "human sexuality and its accompanying love and marriage, and human existence itself" (Okamura 2013: 148). What makes *Exceedingly Barbaric* an interesting critique of colonialism is its attentiveness to both the macro politics and microphysics of colonial lives. From governmentality to domesticity, from patriarchy to sexuality, the novel crafts the entangled stories of colonial expansion, with all its sensibilities, sentiments, and states of distress that haunt and hover the descriptive fringes of colonial histories and its postcolonial legacies.

Finding Sayun is the first feature film on indigenous culture from the perspective of the aboriginal director, Laha Mebow, of the Atayal tribe in northeastern Taiwan. The film begins when the tale of Sayun draws a TV crew consisting of a Taiwanese female reporter and two cameramen from Beijing to the Atayal hamlet. (It is not quite clear from the film why the two men from Beijing were necessary for the narrative.) As the crew interviews local residents and tries to find out more about Sayun's story, they are increasingly attracted to You-Gan, a handsome high school boy and hunter, who does not understand the crew members' interest in the story. (In an earlier scene, You-Gan literally runs away from the crew's camera.) But his grandfather's memories of Sayun, whom he went to school with, revives his interest in the old tribal village, which the villagers had been forced to desert fifty years prior by the Kuomintang after "liberating" Taiwan from the Japanese. Due to concern over his health and old age, not to mention the treacherous and abandoned mountain trails leading to the old village, the grandfather has been prohibited from visiting his village. With the memory of Sayun and his yearning for home stirring, the grandfather is determined to pay a visit to his childhood home. You-Gan, with his friends and the female reporter, then embark on a journey along the hazardous trail to the Atayal home.

3. *Warriors of the Rainbow: Seediq Bale* forms one of the so-called Taiwan trilogy by the director Wei Te-sheng, along with *Cape No. 7* (2006) and *Kano* (2014). These films are all box office hits in Taiwan and have garnered positive reviews abroad.

4. See http://www.epochweekly.com/b5/256/10203p.htm.

5. I don't have any information about the particular Japanese prime minister and the apology that Derrida is thinking of, but my guess is that, since the book was published in 2001, he may be referring to Murayama Tomiichi, the socialist prime minister of Japan from June 1994 to January 1996, who offered apologies for Japanese colonial rule and aggressions to Asian neighbors. The so-called Murayama Statement is officially titled "On the Occasion of the Fiftieth Anniversary of the War's End." Derrida also appears to be overly optimistic about "reparation and a political reorientation"(2001: 31). The exclusion of the emperor from the act of apology is already a concession to the postwar American and Japanese complicity to absolve the emperor of any war crimes and wrongdoings. And if indeed Murayama was the example whom Derrida cites, we should not ignore the fact that, despite his much more reconciliatory attitude than other postwar prime ministers, he presided over the short-lived Asian Women's Fund (1994–2007) that established a private mechanism to compensate the so-called comfort women for their sufferings but again absolved the state of any responsibility for the system of sexual slavery. In November of 2015, McGraw-Hill, publisher of the world history textbook *Traditions and Encounters: A Global Perspective on the Past, Vol. 2*, by the history professors Herbert Ziegler and Jerry Bentley, was contacted by Japan's Consulate General in New York to request the deletion of two paragraphs (i.e., the entire entry) about the comfort women.

Akiyama, Jōji, and Kō Bunyu. 2013. *Manga Chūgoku nyūmon: yakkai na rinjin no kenkyū* [Manga intro to China: The study of a troublesome neighbor]. Tokyo: Asukashinsha.

Allison, Anne. 2013. *Precarious Japan*. Durham, NC: Duke University Press.

Arendt, Hannah. 1963. *Eichmann in Jerusalem: A Report on the Banality of Evil*. London: Penguin.

Badiou, Alain, and Nicolas Truong. 2012. *In Praise of Love*. New York: The New Press.

Berry, Chris. 2006. "Stellar Transit: Bruce Lee's Body or Chinese Masculinity in a Transnational Frame." In *Embodied Modernities: Corporeality, Representation, and Chinese Cultures*, ed. Fran Martin and Larissa Heinrich, 218–34. Honolulu: University of Hawai'i Press.

Billig, Michael. 1995. *Banal Nationalism*. London: Sage.

Bix, Herbert. 2001. *Hirohito and the Making of Modern Japan*. New York: HarperCollins.

Butler, Judith. 1997. *Excitable Speech: A Politics of the Performative*. London: Routledge.

Butler, Judith. 2004. *Precarious Life: The Powers of Mourning and Violence*. London: Verso.

Callahan, William. 2007. "Trauma and Community: The Visual Politics of Chinese Nationalism and Sino-Japanese Relations." *Theory and Event* 10, no. 4. https://muse.jhu.edu/article/230142.

Callahan, William. 2010. *China: The Pessoptimist Nation*. Oxford: Oxford University Press.

Cao Rui. 2018. "Jingri shi shemo yisi" [What is spiritually Japanese?]. *Xuehua News*, February 26. https://www.xuehua.us/2018/02/26/精日是什么意思-曝光人揭秘三类精日圈/zh-tw/.

Chen Duxiu. 1937. *Kangri zhanzheng zhi yiyi* [The meaning of the war of resistance]. Speech given at Huachung University, Wuhan, China, on October 6. https://www.marxists.org/chinese/chenduxiu/mia-chinese-chen-19371006.htm.

Chen Kuan-Hsing. 2000. "The Imperialist Eye: The Cultural Imaginary of a Sub-empire and a Nation-State." Trans. Wang Yiman. *positions: east asia cultures critique* 8, no 1: 9–76.

Chen Kuan-Hsing. 2002. "Why Is 'Great Reconciliation' Impossible? De-Cold War/Decolonization, Or Modernity and Its Tears (Part 1)." *Inter-Asia Cultural Studies* 3, no. 1: 77–99.

Chen Kuan-Hsing. 2010. *Asia as Method: Toward Deimperialization.* Durham, NC: Duke University Press.

Cheong, Sung-hwa. 1991. *The Politics of Anti-Japanese Sentiment in Korea: Japanese–South Korean Relations under American Occupation, 1945–1952.* New York: Greenwood Press.

Ching, Leo T. S. 2001. *Becoming "Japanese": The Politics of Identity Formation in Colonial Taiwan.* Berkeley: University of California Press.

Ching, Leo T. S. 2012. "Colonial Nostalgia or Postcolonial Anxiety: The Dōsan Generation In Between 'Restoration' and 'Defeat.'" In *Sino-Japanese Transculturation: From the Late Nineteenth Century to the End of the Pacific War,* ed. Richard King, Cody Poulton, and Katsuhiko Endo, 211–26. Lanham, MD: Lexington Books.

Cho Han Hae-joang. 2001. "'You Are Entrapped in an Imaginary Well': The Formation of Subjectivity within Compressed Development—a Feminist Critique of Modernity and Korean Culture." *Inter-Asia Cultural Studies* 1, no. 1: 49–69.

Choi, Chungmoo. 2001. "The Politics of War Memories toward Healing." In *Perilous Memories: The Asia-Pacific War,* ed. T. Fujitani, Geoffrey M. While, and Lisa Yoneyama, 395–409. Durham, NC: Duke University Press.

Choi, Chungmoo. 2002. "The Politics of Gender, Aestheticism, and Cultural Nationalism in Sopyonje and the Genealogy." In *Im Kwon-Taek: The Making of a Korean National Cinema,* ed. David E. James and Kyung Hyun Kim, 107–33. Detroit, MI: Wayne State University Press.

Chow, Rey. 2002. *The Protestant Ethnic and the Spirit of Capitalism.* New York: Columbia University Press.

Chow, Rey. 2012. *Entanglements: Or Transmedial Thinking about Capture.* Durham, NC: Duke University Press.

Common History Project [Nicchūkansankoku kyōtsurekishikyōzai iinkai]. 2006. *Mirai wo hiraku rekishi: nihon, chūgoku, kankoku kyōtsuhenshu higashiajia sankoku no kindaishi* [A history that opens to the future: Japan, China, and Korea; The contemporary and modern history of the three East Asian countries]. Tokyo: Kōbunken.

Common History Project [Nicchūkansankoku kyōtsurekishikyōzai iinkai]. 2012a. *Atarashii higashiajia no kingendaishi Vol. 1: kokusai kankei no hendō de yomu* [New modern history of East Asia, vol. 1, Reading changes in international relations]. Tokyo: Nihon hyōronsha.

Common History Project [Nicchūkansankoku kyōtsurekishikyōzai iinkai]. 2012b. *Atarashii higashiajia no kingendaishi Vol. 2: teima de yomu hito to kōryū* [New modern history of East Asia, vol. 2: People and exchanges]. Tokyo: Nihon hyōronsha.

Connery, Christopher. 2001. "On the Continuing Necessity of Anti-Americanism." *Inter-Asia Cultural Studies* 2, no. 3: 399–405.

Davis, Heather, and Paige Sarlin. 2008. "On the Risk of a New Rationality: An Interview with Lauren Berlant and Michael Hardt." *Review in Cultural Theory* 2, no. 3. http://reviewsinculture.com/2012/10/15/on-the-risk-of-a-new-relationality-an-interview-with-lauren-berlant-and-michael-hardt/.

Derrida, Jacques. 2001. *On Cosmopolitanism and Forgiveness*. London: Routledge.

Dirlik, Arif. 1991. "'Past Experience, If Not Forgotten, Is a Guide to the Future'; Or, What Is in a Text? The Politics of History in Chinese-Japanese Relations." *boundary 2* 18, no. 3: 29–58.

Dirlik, Arif. 2002. "Rethinking Colonialism: Globalization, Postcolonialism, and the Nation." *Interventions* 4, no. 3 (January): 428–48.

Dower, John. 2000. *Embracing Defeat: Japan in the Wake of World War II*. New York: W. W. Norton and Company.

Dudden, Alexis. 2014. *Troubled Apologies among Japan, Korea, and the United States*. New York: Columbia University Press.

Escobar, Arturo. 2018. *Designs for the Pluriverse: Radical Independence, Autonomy, and the Making of Worlds*. Durham, NC: Duke University Press.

Fabian, Johannes. 2002. *Time and the Other: How Anthropology Makes Its Object*. New York: Columbia University Press.

"Fact Sheet on Japanese Military 'Comfort Women.'" 2015. *Asia-Pacific Journal*, May 11. https://apjjf.org/-Asia-Pacific-Journal-Feature/4829/article.html.

Fanon, Frantz. 1968. *The Wretched of the Earth*. New York: Grove Press.

Feldman, Noah. 2015. "Apology Isn't Justice for Korean's 'Comfort Women.'" *Bloomberg View*, December 28. https://www.bloomberg.com/opinion/articles/2015-12-28/how-korea-s-deal-with-japan-fails-comfort-women-.

Field, Norma. 1991. *In the Realm of a Dying Emperor: A Portrait of Japan at Century's End*. New York: Pantheon.

Fore, Steve. 2001. "Life Imitates Entertainment: Home and Dislocation in the Films of Jackie Chan." In *At Full Speed: Hong Kong Cinema in a Borderless World*, ed. Esther C. M. Yau, 115–41. Minneapolis: University of Minnesota Press.

Gateward, Frances K. 2007. *Seoul Searching: Culture and Identity in Contemporary Korean Cinema*. Albany: State University of New York Press.

Giddens, Anthony. 1992. *The Transformation of Intimacy: Sexuality, Love, and Eroticism in Modern Societies*. Stanford, CA: Stanford University Press.

Guthrie-Shimizu, Sayuri. 2006. "Lost in Translation and Morphed in Transit: Godzilla in Cold War America." In *In Godzilla's Footsteps: Japanese Pop Culture Icon in the Global Stage*, ed. William M. Tsutsui and Michiko Ito, 51–62. New York: Palgrave Macmillan.

Halliday, Jon, and Gavan McCormack. 1973. *Japanese Imperialism Today: "Co-Prosperity in Greater East Asia"*. New York: Monthly Review Press.

Hanasaki, Kōhei. 2000. "Decolonialization and Assumption of War Responsibility." *Inter-Asia Cultural Studies* 1, no. 1: 71–83.

Hanasaki, Kōhei. 2001. *Aidentiti to kyōsei no tetsugaku* [The philosophy of identity and co-vivality]. Tokyo: Heibonsha Library.

Hara, Kazuo, dir. 1987. *Yukiyukite shingun* [The emperor's naked army marches on]. Tokyo: Shissō Purodakushon.

Hardt, Michael. 2011. "For Love or Money." *Cultural Anthropology* 26, no. 4: 676–82.

Hoaglund, Linda. 2003. "Stubborn Legacies of War: Japanese Devils in Sarajevo." *Asia-Pacific Journal/Japan Focus* 1, no. 10. https://apjjf.org/-Linda-Hoaglund/1822/article.html.

Honda, Katsuichi. 1981. *Chūgoku no tabi* [Travels in China]. Tokyo: Asahi shimbun shuppan.

Huang Chih-huei (Huang Zhihui). 2004. "Zhan-hou Taiwan de 'Riben wenhua lun' shuwu zhong xianxiande 'dui-wu zhong xianxiande 'ihui), Modernity and its Tears (Part 1)," Ri guan" [Attitudes toward Japan manifested in postwar books from Taiwan on "Discourse on Japanese Culture"]. *Ya-Tai yanjiu luntan* [Forum for Asia-Pacific Debate] 26: 94–118.

Huang, Zheping. 2018. "Cosplaying as Japanese Soldiers Could Become Illegal in China." *Quartz*, April 26. https://qz.com/1262615/china-considers-punishing-those-who-glorify-japanese-militarism-in-a-new-heroes-and-martyrs-protection-law/.

Jameson, Fredric. 1991. *Postmodernism, Or, the Cultural Logic of Late Capitalism*. Durham, NC: Duke University Press.

Jameson, Fredric. 1995. *The Geopolitical Aesthetic: Cinema and Space in the World System*. Bloomington: Indiana University Press.

"Japanese PM Stirs Up Trouble with 'Comfort Women' Remark." 2012. *Chosun Ilbo* (English edition), March 28.

Jung, Baek Soo. 2007. *Koroniarizumu no kokufuku: kankoku kindai bunka ni okeru datsu shokuminchi-ka eno dotei* [Overcoming colonialism: The process of decolonization in modern Korean culture]. Tokyo: Sofukan.

Karatani, Kōjin. 2014. *The Structure of World History: From Modes of Production to Modes of Exchange*. Trans. Michael Bourdaghs. Durham, NC: Duke University Press.

Kato, M. T. 2007. *From Kung Fu to Hip Hop: Globalization, Revolution, and Popular Culture*. Albany: State University of New York Press.

Katō Norihiro. 1997. *Haisengoron* [On war defeat]. Tokyo: Kōdansha.

Katō Norihiro. 2010. *Sayōnara, Gojira-tachi: Sengo Kara Tōku Hanarete*. Tokyo: Iwanami Shoten.

Kim, Hang. 2016. "Universalism and Colonialism: Reconsidering Postwar Democracy in Japan." *Inter-Asia Cultural Studies* 17, no. 3: 481–95.

Kim, Kyung Hyun. 2004. *The Remasculinization of Korean Cinema*. Durham, NC: Duke University Press.

Kim, Nami. 2012. "Marking the 1,000th Wednesday Demonstration." *Feminist Studies in Religion*, January 14. http://www.fsrinc.org/blog/marking-1000th -wednesday-demonstration.

Kim, Soyoung. 2006. "Do Not Include Me in Your Us: Peppermint Candy and the Politics of Difference." *Korea Journal* 46, no. 1: 60–83.

Kim-Gibson, Dai Sil. 1997. "They Are Our Grandmas." *positions: east asia cultures critique* 5, no. 1: 255–74.

Kō, Eitetsu. 1999. *Taiwan bunka saikōchiku no hikari to kage (1945–1947): Lu Xun shisō juyō no ikue* [The light and shadow of the reconstruction of Taiwan culture (1945–1947): Acceptance of Lu Xun's thoughts]. Tokyo: Sōdosha.

Ko, Yu-fen. 2003. "Consuming Differences: 'Hello Kitty' and the Identity Crisis in Taiwan." *Postcolonial Studies* 6, no. 2: 175–89.

Kobayashi Yoshinori. 2000. *Shin-gōmanizumu sengen. Special Taiwan ron* [A manifesto of the new pride: A special theory of Taiwan]. Tokyo: Shōgakukan.

Koschmann, Victor J. 2006. "National Subjectivity and the Uses of Atonement in the Age of Recession." In *Japan after Japan: Social and Cultural Life from the Recessionary 1990s to the Present*, ed. Tomiko Yoda and Harry Harootunian, 122–41. Durham, NC: Duke University Press.

Kushner, Barak. 2006. "Gojira as Japan's First Postwar Media Event." In *In Godzilla's Footsteps: Japanese Pop Culture Icon on the Global Stage*, ed. William M. Tsutsui and Michiko Ito, 41–50. New York: Palgrave Macmillan.

Kushner, Barak. 2015. *Men to Devils, Devils to Men: Japanese War Crimes and Chinese Justice*. Cambridge, MA: Harvard University Press. Kindle.

Kwon, Nayoung Aimee. 2015. *Intimate Empire: Collaboration and Colonial Modernity in Korea and Japan*. Durham, NC: Duke University Press.

Laha Mebow (Chen, Chieh-yao), dir. 2010. *Buyiyang de yueguang* (Finding Sayun). Hua-Ying Entertainment.

Lee, Hyunjung, and Younghan Cho. 2009. "Performing Nation-ness in South Korea during the 2002 Korea-Japan World Cup." *Korea Journal* 49 no. 3: 93–120.

Lee, Woo-young. 2016. "'Comfort Women' Statues Resonate with Koreans." *The Korea Herald*, March 6. http://www.koreaherald.com/view.php?ud =20160303000844

Leys, Ruth. 2007. *From Guilt to Shame: Auschwitz and After*. Princeton, NJ: Princeton University Press.

Lo, Kwai-Cheung. 1996. "Muscles and Subjectivity: A Short History of the Masculine Body in Hong Kong Popular Culture." *Camera Obscura* 13, no. 3 (September): 104–25.

Lowe, Lisa. 2006. "The Intimacies of Four Continents." In *Haunted by Empire: Geographies of Intimacy in North America History*, ed. Ann Stoler, 191–212. Durham, NC: Duke University Press.

Manto, Saddat Hasan. 2008. *Kingdom's End: Selected Stories*. New York: Penguin Global.

Marotti, William A. 2013. *Money, Trains, and Guillotines: Art and Revolution in 1960s Japan*. Durham, NC: Duke University Press.

McGregor, Katharine. 2016. "Emotions and Activism for Former So-called 'Comfort Women' of the Japanese Occupation of the Netherlands East Indies." *Women's Studies International Forum* 54: 67–78.

Mitchell, W. J. T. 2000. "What Sculpture Wants: Placing Antony Gormley." In *Antony Gormley: Blind Light*, ed. Anthony Vidler, Susan Stewart, and W. J. T. Mitchell. London: Phaidon. http://www.antonygormley.com/resources/download-text/id/114.

Miyoshi, Masao. 1991. *Off Center: Power and Culture Relations between Japan and the United States*. Cambridge, MA: Harvard University Press.

Mizoguchi Yūzō. 2005. "Hannichi demo: Doyū rekishi no medemiruka" [Anti-Japan demonstration: How to see through the eye of history]. *Gendai Shiso* 33: 144–51.

Mori Yoshio. 2001. *Taiwan/nihon-rensasuru Koroniarizumu* [Colonialism connecting Taiwan and Japan]. Tokyo: Impact Shuppansha.

Morris-Suzuki, Tessa. 2005. *The Past within Us: Media, Memory, History*. London: Verso.

Napier, Susan J. 1993. "Panic Sites: The Japanese Imaginations of Disaster from Godzilla to Akira." *Journal of Japanese Studies* 19, no. 2: 327–51.

Natali, Marcos Piason. 2004. "History and the Politics of Nostalgia." *Iowa Journal of Cultural Studies* 5, no. 1. http://www.uiowa.edu/~ijcs/nostalgia/nostfe1.htm.

Nishimura, Kohyu. 2004. *Hannichi no kozo: Chugoku, kankoku, kitachosen wo aotteiru no wa dareka* [The structure of anti-Japan: Who is flaming China, South and North Korea?]. Tokyo: PHP Kenkyusho.

Nozawa, Shunsuke. 2013. "Characterization." *Semiotic Review* 3. https://www.semioticreview.com/ojs/index.php/sr/article/view/16/15.

Nussbaum, Martha Craven. 2013. *Political Emotions: Why Love Matters for Justice*. Cambridge, MA: Harvard University Press.

O'Day, Robin. 2015. "Differentiating SEALDs from Freeters and Precariats: The Politics of Youth Movements in Contemporary Japan." *Asia-Pacific Journal* 13, no. 37. https://apjjf.org/-Robin-O_Day/4376.

Oguma, Eiji. 2004. *Minshu to aikoku: Sengo nihon no nashonarizumu to kōkyōsei* [Democracy and patriotism: Postwar Japanese nationalism and the public]. Tokyo: Shinyōsha.

Okamoto, Tomoko. 2013. "Tsushima Yūko 'amari ni yabanna' ron: sei to shi no rondo" [On Tsushima Yūko's *Amari ni yabanna*: A rondo of life and death]. *Modern Japanese Literary Studies* 89: 139–53.

Otsuki, Tomoe. 2016. "Reinventing Nagasaki: The Christianization of Nagasaki and the Revival of an Imperial Legacy in Postwar Japan." *Inter-Asia Cultural Studies* 17, no. 3: 395–415.

Park, Yuha. 2006. *Wakai no tame ni: kyōkasho, ianfu, tokuto* [For reconciliation: Text books, "comfort women," and Dokto]. Tokyo: Heibonsha.

Prashad, Vijay. 2001. *Everybody Was Kung Fu Fighting: Afro-Asian Connections and the Myth of Cultural Purity*. Boston, MA: Beacon.

Qiu, Jack Linchuan. 2004. "The Internet in China: Technologies of Freedom in a

Statist Society." In *The Network Society: A Cross-Cultural Perspective*, ed. Manuel Castells, 99–124. Northampton, MA: Edward Elgar.

Reddy, William M. 2012. *The Making of Romantic Love: Longing and Sexuality in Europe, South Asia, and Japan, 900–1200 CE*. Chicago: University of Chicago Press.

Sakai, Naoki, Brett de Bary, and Toshio Iyotani. 2005. *Deconstructing Nationality*. Ithaca, NY: East Asia Program, Cornell University.

Sakamoto, Rumi, and Matt Allen. 2007. "Hating 'the Korean Wave': Comic Books: A Sign of New Nationalism in Japan?" *Asia-Pacific Journal* 5, no. 10. https://apjjf .org/-Rumi-Sakamoto/2535/article.html.

Students Emergency Actions for Liberal Democracy. 2016. *Nihon X Hong Kong X Taiwan Wakamono Ha Akiramenai: Kokkyo Wo Koeta "gakusei Undo" No Rentai Ha Kanoka* [Youths never give up—Japan, Hong Kong, and Taiwan: Is a transnational student solidarity possible?]. Tokyo: Ohta Shuppan.

Shih, Shu-Mei. 2003. "Globalisation and the (In)Significance of Taiwan." *Postcolonial Studies* 6, no 2: 143–53.

Shōji, Sōichi. 1940. *Chin fujin* [Madam Chen]. Tokyo: Tsūbunkaku.

Soh, Chunghee Sarah. 2008. *The Comfort Women: Sexual Violence and Postcolonial Memory in Korea and Japan*. Chicago: University of Chicago Press.

Spurr, David. 1993. *The Rhetoric of Empire: Colonial Discourse in Journalism, Travel Writing, and Imperial Administration*. Durham, NC: Duke University Press.

Starrs, Roy. 2001. *Asian Nationalism in an Age of Globalization*. New York: Routledge.

Stoler, Ann. 2002. *Carnal Knowledge and Imperial Power: Race and the Intimate in Colonial Rule*. Berkeley: University of California Press.

Sun Ge. 2010. "How Does Asia Mean? (Part I)." *Inter-Asia Cultural Studies* 1, no. 1:13–47.

Sun Ge, Kuan-Hsing Chen and Youngseo Paik, eds. 2006. *Posuto higashi ajia* [Post–East Asia]. Tokyo: Sakuhin sha.

Sun Shen, ed. 1995. *Kangzhan mingqu 100 sho* [100 war of resistance songs]. Zhejiang: Zhejiang Wenyi Chubanshe.

Takeda, Masaya. 2005. *The Portraits of "Guizi"*. Tokyo: Shueisha.

Tanaka, Yuki. 2007. "Oda Makoto, Beheiren, and 14 August 1945: Humanitarian Wrath against Indiscriminate Bombing." *The Asia-Pacific Journal/Japan Focus* 5, no. 9. https://apjjf.org/-Yuki-Tanaka/2532/article.html.

Tsushima, Yūko. 2008. *Amari ni yabanna* [Exceedingly Barbaric]. Tokyo: Kodansha.

Tudor, Andrew. 1989. *Monsters and Mad Scientists: A Cultural History of the Horror Movie*. New York: Blackwell.

Vijayan, Suchitra. 2014. "Rwanda and the NY Times: On Those Images by Pieter Hugo Pairing Perpetrators and Victims of the 1994 Genocide." *Africa Is a Country*, April 25. https://africasacountry.com/2014/04/rwanda-the-genocide -must-live-on.

Wang, Chih-ming. 2013. *Transpacific Articulations: Student Migration and the Remaking of Asian America*. Honolulu: University of Hawai'i Press.

Watson, Burton. 2003. *Mozi: Basic Writings*. New York: Columbia University Press.

Wu Zhuoliu, and Ioannis Mentzas. 2006. *Orphan of Asia*. New York: Columbia University Press.

Xu, Gary G. 2007. *Sinascape: Contemporary Chinese Cinema*. Lanham, MD: Rowman and Littlefield.

Yamano Sharin. 2005. *Kenkanryū* [Hating the Korean wave]. Tokyo: Shinyūsha.

Yang, Hyunah. 1997. "Revisiting the Issue of Korean 'Military Comfort Women': The Question of Truth and Positionality." *positions: east asia cultures critique* 5, no. 1: 51–72.

Yomota Inuhiko. 2005. *Burusu Ri: Ri Shiuron no eikō to kodoku* [Bruce Lee: The glory and solitude of Li Xioa-long]. Tokyo: Shōbunsha.

Yoneyama, Lisa. 2016. *Cold War Ruins: Transpacific Critique of American Justice and Japanese War Crimes*. Durham, NC: Duke University Press.

Yoshida, Takashi. 2006. *The Making of the "Rape of Nanking": History and Memory in Japan, China, and the United States*. New York: Oxford University Press.

Yoshimi, Shun'ya, and David Buist. 2003. "'America' as Desire and Violence: Americanization in Postwar Japan and Asia during the Cold War." *Inter-Asia Cultural Studies* 4, no. 3: 433–50.

Žižek, Slavoj. 2006. "Is This Digital Democracy, or a New Tyranny of Cyberspace?" *Guardian*, December 30. http://www.guardian.co.uk/commentisfree/2006/dec/30/comment.media.

The Emperor's Naked Army Marches On (film), 55–56

The Murmuring (film), 61, 66, 68, 70, 71, 75

Treaty on Basic Relations between Japan and the Republic of Korea (1965), 60

Tsushima, Yūko, 18, 120–21, 123, 124, 126, 127

Tunnel Warfare (film), 43, 44, 45

umbrella movement, 132

Ushida Yoshimasa, 133, 134, 135

Vijayan, Suchitra, 129–30

waishengren (mainlanders and their descendants), 84, 94

Women's International War Crimes Tribunal, 74, 147n15

Wong, Joshua, 133, 134, 135

Yamano Sharin, 9, 108

Yan Lianke, 3

Yasukuni Shrine, 80

Yoneyama, Lisa, 56, 74–75

Yoshimi, Shun'ya, 7